big fish, little fish

A MinnowKnits Book

Also by Jil Eaton

MinnowKnits
Uncommon Clothes to Knit for Kids

MinnowKnits, Too
More Uncommon Knits for Kids,
Big and Small

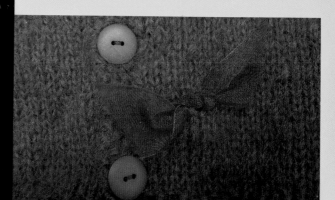

big fish, little fish

A MinnowKnits Book

QuickKnits for Kids & Grown-Ups

Jil Eaton

Contemporary Books

A Division of The McGraw-Hill Companies

Library of Congress Cataloging-in-Publication Data

Eaton, Jil.
     Big fish, little fish : quickknits for kids and grown-ups / Jil Eaton ; photography by
Nina Fuller.
        p.   cm.
     ISBN 0-8092-2430-5 (hardcover)
     ISBN 0-07-139611-X (paperback)
     1. Knitting—Patterns   2. Children's clothing   3. Clothing and dress   I. Title.
TT825.E2797   2000
746.46'0432—dc21
                                     00-31406
                                        CIP

Contemporary Books

A Division of The **McGraw·Hill** *Companies*

1 2 3 4 5 6 7 8 9 0 SSI/SSI 1 0 9 8 7 6 5 4 3 2

ISBN 0-8092-2430-5 (hardcover)
ISBN 0-07-139611-X (paperback)

This book was set in Sabon
Printed and bound by Star Standard Industries

Editorial and production direction by Anne Knudsen
Art direction and cover design by Kim Bartko
Book design by Hespenheide Design
Project editing by Kristen Eberhard
Manufacturing direction by Pat Martin

Pattern design by Jil Eaton
Technical writing and editing by Carla Scott
Pattern proofing and editing by Judith Shangold
Illustrations by Jil Eaton
Learn-to-knit illustrations by Joni Coniglio
Schematics by Elizabeth Berry
Photography by Nina Van Brocklyn Fuller
Art direction for photography by Jil Eaton
Styling by Merle Hagelin, Isabel Smiles, Jil Eaton
Knitting by Nita Young, Joan Cassidy, Carol Gillis, Starr Moore, Audrey Lewis, Peggy Lewis,
Leslie Scanlon, Veronica Manning, Charlotte Parry, Ellen L'Esperance, Janice Bye, Lucinda
Heller, Connie Gemmer, Christina Astrachan

McGraw-Hill books are available at special quantity discounts to use as premiums and sales
promotions, or for use in corporate training programs. For more information, please write to
the Director of Special Sales, Professional Publishing, McGraw-Hill, Two Penn Plaza, New
York, NY 10121-2298. Or contact your local bookstore.

*Every effort has been made to be accurate and complete with all the information in this book.
The publisher and the author cannot, however, be responsible for differences in knitters' abili-
ties, typographical errors, techniques, tools or conditions, or any resulting damages, mistakes, or losses. Minnowknits hand-knitting patterns may not be knit for resale.*

To my father, Russell Edison Lord, who lives among the stars.

A most extraordinary Big Fish, my father gave me the courage to try again, to laugh at myself, to sing out loud, to fly. Loving, handsome, smart, and generous, he also taught me integrity; I strive to live up to his dreams.

Contents

Preface

When I was seven, an enormous box arrived from J. C. Best in New York City, filled with a soft black velvet party dress that felt like a cloud. It had tulle and chiffon underskirts, a smocked bodice, and elegant full sleeves. It was a dress for a princess, caught behind the waist with a silky satin bow falling way below the knees. But then came the best part: a short black angora sweater to wear with this wonderful dress, with delicate pearl buttons and grosgrain trim, knit by my mother. She had knit a matching one for herself, too: a small cardigan for evenings and holidays needing a little cozy sparkle. Imagine the luxury of dressing like your beautiful and young mother, being a princess for hours on end. As my mother knit those sweaters, she created memories, stitch by stitch. So, perfectly matching or simply side by side, *Big Fish, Little Fish* makes creating such memories possible.

Over the years I have had constant requests from knitters, grandmothers, shop owners, and even my models for MinnowKnits patterns in all sizes, not just for kids. So with an ever-watchful eye on design and proportion, here is a brand new collection of patterns, sized to fit everyone in your life, from toddlers on up! You'll find hats and sox and mittens and sweaters and jackets and waistcoats and pullovers, all in clear wonderful colors, beautiful yarns, and chic and charming designs. From party clothes to rumble-tumble sportswear, here is an easy-to-knit collection that's fit for all. Mix and match to your heart's delight.

Sizing usually begins with 2, 4, 6, and 8 years for the children's patterns and then skips to small, medium, and large for adults. You will find that many patterns become unisex, given the sizing variations; simply measure the intended person, and knit! And usually a 10 year old can wear the small adult size, making the range complete. It has been quite a leap, since garments fit very differently on adults, even given identical style. Ah, what a challenge!

This collection is organized by category, including sporting types, party clothes, and accessories. There are knitting tips for each garment, tidbits, and ideas. And please, please measure! If you do your gauge and measure the person you are knitting for or a well-fitting garment, you will always have a perfect fit.

Each garment is photographed on both kids and adults, in various combinations, such as mother and daughter, father and son, brother and sister, friends, cousins, and one even on an expectant mother before and after the baby's arrival. I've presented the garments in all imaginable combinations, so you can cre-

ate your own. Photographs were shot both on location and in the studio, showing the garments formally and right in the midst of the action. I love to imagine all of these garments in their many shapes and sizes and colors, made on flying needles for all of your favorites, both big and little.

Remember, when we are knitting, all is right with the world!

Jil Eaton

Trade Secrets

Knit, knit, knit! I knit for every reason imaginable, anywhere and all the time. Knitting is magic, a Zenlike way to calm down and meditate, a simple way to find clear just-for-oneself time. Often I hear people say they don't have time to knit, yet I find that some of the busiest women I know are the best knitters! Our intense and extremely challenging lives call for a creative yet relaxing and productive activity. I always keep two or more projects in the works, to prevent boredom and allow portability. I usually have a first-thing-in-the-morning project, some simple evening-at-home projects, and small, easy-to-carry hats, mittens, or sox on my needles at all times. Who can watch an old movie, wait for the dentist, or survive the vacation drive without her knitting? Here are a few of my trade secrets and technical tips. I hope you will knit, knit, knit!

KNITTING KIT

When I begin my knitting classes there are a few tricks and tools I recommend to promote successful projects. I have learned over the years that keeping an organized easy-to-see, clear zippered pouch full of knitting tools is a necessity. A completely clear pouch is best and can be found in most drugstores. In your knitting kit, you will need the following:

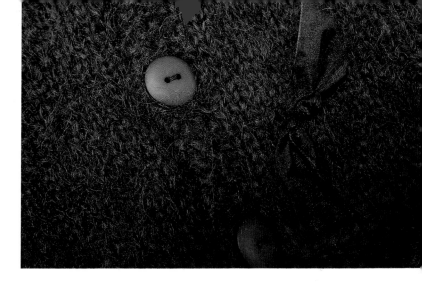

Small, sharp scissors

Yarn needles (I like Chibi needles with bent tips best)

Measuring tape (I like the retractable kind)

Yarn T-pins and safety pins for marking or holding dropped stitches

Stitch holders, both short and long

Stitch markers (split-rings are my favorites, as they can be easily moved)

Cable needles (my favorites are straight)

Small calculator (invaluable!)

Point protectors, both large and small, to keep your work on the needles

Row counter

Needle/gauge ruler

Crochet hooks, one small, one large

Pen and notebook, for taking notes, figuring, and designing

STUDIO SUPPLIES

I also keep knitting supplies in my studio or home. These essentials will really make a difference in your knitting life!

KNITTING BAG OR BASKET

I have many knitting bags, usually one in each room of my house, two for traveling, and larger ones for the studio. I love lightweight mesh bags for traveling, as the yarn can get heavy and baskets can be bulky. Use whatever carryall you like, but dedicate it to your projects and you'll always have everything at hand.

NEEDLES

You will, sooner or later, want a complete set of needles, with doubles in your favorite sizes. I use different needles for various projects depending on the yarn or garment.

Basic Needles

Swallow casein needles are wonderful, warm in your hand, silent, and available in 9″ / 23 cm, 12″ / 30 cm, and 14″ / 35 cm. They are fabulous and perfect for basic straight 2-needle knitting. I always favor the shortest needle possible because it puts less strain on your wrists. Swallow needles come in beautiful tortoise, as well as in vibrant colors, in the 12″ / 30 cm length.

knit stitch. The cable cast-on is a variation of the first method and is used to form a sturdy, yet elastic edge.

For your first project, the ChinChilly neck-warmer is perfect, because it is an easy way to master knitting before going on to the more advanced stitches. There is no shaping in this pattern, and as it is all done in garter stitch, or knit every row, it will give you great practice knitting. You might want to try this project in a plain, soft, chunky yarn so the stitches will be easy to see. And, finally, you will learn how to bind off, which is necessary to complete any project. By binding off, you fasten off all remaining stitches so that they will not unravel.

SLIP KNOT

1. Hold the yarn in your left hand, leaving a short length free. Wrap the yarn from the skein into a circle and bring the yarn from below and up through the center of the circle. Insert the needle under this strand as shown.
2. Pull on both the short and long ends to tighten the knot on the needle.

This section takes you through the basic elements of knitting. I have described two types of cast-ons, the knit on cast-on and the cable cast-on. Once you have learned the knitting-on method, you have actually learned the basic

KNITTING KIT

When I begin my knitting classes there are a few tricks and tools I recommend to promote successful projects. I have learned over the years that keeping an organized easy-to-see, clear zippered pouch full of knitting tools is a necessity. A completely clear pouch is best and can be found in most drugstores. In your knitting kit, you will need the following:

Small, sharp scissors
Yarn needles (I like Chibi needles with bent tips best)
Measuring tape (I like the retractable kind)
Yarn T-pins and safety pins for marking or holding dropped stitches
Stitch holders, both short and long
Stitch markers (split-rings are my favorites, as they can be easily moved)
Cable needles (my favorites are straight)
Small calculator (invaluable!)
Point protectors, both large and small, to keep your work on the needles
Row counter
Needle/gauge ruler
Crochet hooks, one small, one large
Pen and notebook, for taking notes, figuring, and designing

STUDIO SUPPLIES

I also keep knitting supplies in my studio or home. These essentials will really make a difference in your knitting life!

KNITTING BAG OR BASKET

I have many knitting bags, usually one in each room of my house, two for traveling, and larger ones for the studio. I love lightweight mesh bags for traveling, as the yarn can get heavy and baskets can be bulky. Use whatever carryall you like, but dedicate it to your projects and you'll always have everything at hand.

NEEDLES

You will, sooner or later, want a complete set of needles, with doubles in your favorite sizes. I use different needles for various projects depending on the yarn or garment.

Basic Needles

Swallow casein needles are wonderful, warm in your hand, silent, and available in 9″ / 23 cm, 12″ / 30 cm, and 14″ / 35 cm. They are fabulous and perfect for basic straight 2-needle knitting. I always favor the shortest needle possible because it puts less strain on your wrists. Swallow needles come in beautiful tortoise, as well as in vibrant colors, in the 12″ / 30 cm length.

Circular Needles

Addi Turbo circular knitting needles are billed as the "amazing turbos," which is perfectly accurate! Made of silver-plated brass that is easy in your hands, soft, and quiet, Addi needles actually speed up your knitting time. The soft cords let stitches glide quickly along the needles, without snags or catches to slow you down. I use the Addi circulars often, simply working back and forth rather than around when appropriate. Addi Turbo circulars are sized from 12″ / 30 cm to 60″ / 150 cm, from US 0 (UK 14, 2 mm) to US 10 (UK 40, 6 mm) in size, easily accommodating any project. They are so smooth, fast to work with, quiet, and flexible—just a joy to have in your hands.

Double Pointed Needles

For these pokey pointed sets, I love both Swallow casein and bamboo. They are as light as air and stay put as you rotate your work. I always carry some in my knitting kit, for easy emergency repair and temporary stitch holders.

NEEDLE CASES

If you begin using needle cases, your needles will be in one place and accessible when you need them. Cases for both straight and circular needles are readily available in knitting shops, in a variety of styles and sizes. Whatever your preference, get some cases and get organized!

KNITTING NOTEBOOK

All my students are required to keep a three-ring binder to organize patterns and projects. Clear three-ring pages that open at the top are perfect for keeping the pattern, notes, and a small amount of the remaining yarn from a project. The yarn is perfect for later repairs,

and the notebook makes a keepsake diary of your projects. You'll be surprised how fast your projects mount up and how much fun it is to remember the garments long after they've left your hands.

YARN WINDER

A table-mounted yarn winder is a great luxury that can be found in your favorite knitting shop or catalog. This can save you hours of time winding hanks of yarn, unless of course you love that yarn-winding ritual, too!

KNITTING LIGHTS

Last, but not least, good light is essential, and I love the kind of lights you can pull down over your work. Everything from old apothecary brass standing lamps to sleek modern designs work, and I have a dedicated knitting light in every room. A high-intensity but adjustable light will save you many hours of mistakes and headaches.

KNITTING TO FIT

A workshop I present when I travel to shows and fiber festivals is called "Gauge, Gauge, Gauge . . . Knitting to Fit." My mantra, the backbone of my design classes, and the most important thing you can do if you want your garments to fit properly is gauge. If you want your garments to fit, just do your swatch!

As you progress with your talents, you will find that knitting the gauge swatch is a very creative part of the project—the point where you make all your design decisions for each particular garment. My colors are meant as a starting point. You may delight in discovering your own new color combinations.

GAUGE SWATCH

A gauge swatch takes only a short time to knit but gives you the information you need to knit a piece that will fit the way you want and expect. Your gauge swatch then becomes part of your knitting history and gives you an extra bit of yarn for emergencies.

Your gauge, or the correct number of stitches per inch or centimeter and the correct number of rows called for in the pattern, is crucial to the success of your knitting project. For instance, knitting at even a half-stitch off gauge will make a significant difference in the final measurement of your garment. If the pattern calls for 100 stitches at 5 stitches to the inch/centimeter, and you are actually getting 5.5 stitches to the inch/centimeter, your sweater will measure 18″ / 45 cm instead of 20″ / 50 cm. Two inches /5 centimeters is a big difference, and the larger the garment, the larger the discrepancy!

Using the needles suggested in the pattern, cast on the correct number of stitches to make a 4″ / 10 cm swatch, plus 6 stitches. Knit 3 rows. Always knit 3 stitches at the beginning and end of every row, and work straight in the pattern stitches called for until the piece measures 4″ / 10 cm, then knit 3 rows and bind off. Lay the swatch on a flat, smooth surface. Measure inside the garter stitch frame; you should have 4″ / 10 cm exactly. If your swatch is too big, or you have too few stitches per inch/centimeter, change to a needle one size smaller. If your swatch is too small, or there are too many stitches per inch/centimeter, change to the next larger needles. Changing one size at a time, keep going until you get the correct gauge.

I consistently knit fast and loose and almost always use needles one size smaller than those recommended in the pattern or on the yarn ball band. Remember, these are recommendations only, as we all knit differently with various needles and yarns. Always do your gauge with the needles you will be using for the project, too; there can be a difference in gauge among plastic, metal, or bamboo needles on the exact same yarn! And check your gauge again after working a few inches/ centimeters, just to be sure you're getting the gauge. Just do it; you'll be happy you did.

ROW COUNTING

If you count your rows, you will have a perfectly matching front and back or two exact sleeves. I always include row counts in my gauge section for every pattern, and you can always count based on the garment chart. If you stretch one piece to match another, the resulting pull will bother you when the garment is finished. My motto is, "when in doubt, tear it out" if it's not perfect. So count your rows for perfect results and easy finishing.

MADE TO MEASURE

Always measure the individual you are knitting for! This may seem simplistic, but I have found that often the simplest steps get overlooked. It is very easy to alter a pattern, making shorter or longer sleeves or bodice, and specific lengths make knitting easy. When knitting sleeves from the shoulder down, as I usually do, make any length adjustments in the bottom half of the sleeve. If the lucky individual being knit for is not available, measure a garment that fits that person comfortably. For children or adults, I recommend knitting a size up if the measurements fall between sizes because children grow at an alarming rate and adults usually enjoy an easy fit! My template is generous, and many of my patterns are QK™, or QuickKnit, quick and simple to knit; even so, you may be surprised by the growth rate of your favorite kid.

When I do workshops and pass out the measuring tapes, everyone groans and giggles. But steady on, and measure up. Copy the body charts for each project, and keep your measurements in your knitting notebook for easy reference. Note that the patterns in the heavier weight yarns in this book often include selvage stitches on each side. These stitches are not included in final measurements, as they are taken up in the seam.

If you are lengthening a garment to fit an individual, make sure you adjust your yardage as well. Our yardage counts are done from the actual sample garments, so you must get extra yarn for larger alterations.

MEASURE UP!

The following tips will help you measure. Along with getting your gauge, accurate measuring is a giant step toward ensuring a good fit.

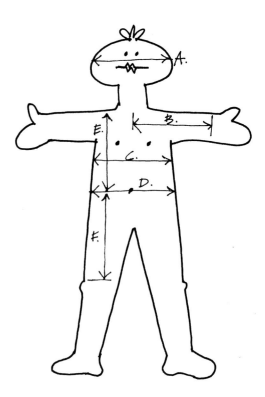

A. For hats, measure the widest part of the head, just above the ears.

B. For the CBS, or center-back-sleeve, measure from the middle of the back straight across to the wrist. This figure will tell you how to adjust the sleeve length, no matter what the design.

C. The chest measurement is probably the most important. Measure around the chest about 1″ / 2.5 cm down from the arm. You might also want to measure a garment that fits the individual comfortably around the chest as well, to aid in finding the correct size.

D. Waist measurement.

E. Shoulder to waist shows the torso length, useful for adjustments in overall garment length.

F. For tunics or longer sweaters, knowing this measurement lets you knit the garment accordingly.

THE RIGHT STUFF

I *always* use the most beautiful yarns I can find, and I believe you should always honor your handwork with the best in materials. I love wool for its warmth, elasticity, durability, and ability to hold beautiful dyes. Cottons now are really great, holding their shapes and colors. Cotton breathes and is comfortable in a great range of weather and climates. It is cool and durable, perfect for long-wearing garments. And the new blends and synthetic chenilles are fabulous.

My patterns are always generic, with the needed amounts for every garment given in yards and meters. You can substitute yarn colors and weights by doing just a bit of math, and your yarn shops can easily help you. I give the yarns that I have used for each knitted sample, so you can find the exact colors and weights; you also might want to experiment, choosing your own creative palette. But *always* use the very best yarns you can afford, in natural fibers and blends. Yarns today are wonderful, washable, and durable, just the thing for heirlooms.

FINISHING

Finish in the morning, in good light, on a flat surface. Finishing the knitting is one thing, but finishing the actual garment is another complete task, requiring rested concentration and attention to detail. We all want to quickly sew up a garment the minute it is off the needles, but good finishing can mean the difference between a beautiful piece and a mediocre effort, so wait until you're fresh and able.

I usually design sweaters with sleeves knit from the shoulder down, using a knitted shoulder seam bind-off. This technique is worked with *wrong sides facing*, resulting in a neat seam on the outside of the shoulder ridge. This seam finishing gives the shoulder stability, while making a design statement.

Tip: When you are adding colors or the next ball of yarn, always leave a 6″ / 15 cm length. This will make the weaving-in at the end much easier.

BLOCKING

When your knitting is complete, weave in all the loose tails of yarn on each piece. Cover each piece with two damp towels, one under and one over, pinning pieces in place. Or pin to a blocking board, which is available through catalogs and yarn shops. Lightly steam at the appropriate setting, and dry flat on a towel, rack, or a blocking board/table if you have one. Blocking usually improves the look of your garment, as long as it is done gently, without mashing down the fibers.

LAUNDERING

Gauge swatches come in very handy for testing washability, following the yarn label instructions. I also have found that many yarns are machine washable, if you put them on a very gentle cycle in tepid water in a small mesh bag, which holds their shape and gets them really clean. For wool, you can also use a no-rinse sweater soap, such as Eucalan, available at fine yarn shops. Fill your washer with tepid (not cold) water, and add the laundry product. Soak the garment for 10 minutes; then go directly to the spin cycle, spin, remove, and block as usual.

If you take care of your hand-knits, they will take care of you for many years!

This section takes you through the basic elements of knitting. I have described two types of cast-ons, the knit on cast-on and the cable cast-on. Once you have learned the knitting-on method, you have actually learned the basic knit stitch. The cable cast-on is a variation of the first method and is used to form a sturdy, yet elastic edge.

For your first project, the ChinChilly neckwarmer is perfect, because it is an easy way to master knitting before going on to the more advanced stitches. There is no shaping in this pattern, and as it is all done in garter stitch, or knit every row, it will give you great practice knitting. You might want to try this project in a plain, soft, chunky yarn so the stitches will be easy to see. And, finally, you will learn how to bind off, which is necessary to complete any project. By binding off, you fasten off all remaining stitches so that they will not unravel.

SLIP KNOT

1. Hold the yarn in your left hand, leaving a short length free. Wrap the yarn from the skein into a circle and bring the yarn from below and up through the center of the circle. Insert the needle under this strand as shown.
2. Pull on both the short and long ends to tighten the knot on the needle.

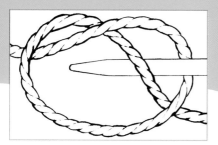

Step 1 Slip knot

Step 1 Cast on

Step 2 Slip knot

Step 2 Cast on

CAST ON

1. Hold the needle with the slip knot in your left hand and the empty needle in your right hand. Insert the right needle from front to back under the left needle and through the stitch. With the yarn in your right hand, wrap the yarn around the right needle as shown.
2. With the tip of the right needle, pull the wrap through the stitch on the left needle and bring it to the front.
3. Slip the new stitch off of the left needle and onto the right needle. Repeat steps 1 to 3 for a simple knit on cast-on. (For an alternate, more advanced method, continue on to step 4.)
4. Insert the right needle between the first two stitches on the left needle and wrap the yarn around the needle as shown. Repeat steps 2 to 4 for the alternate method, cable cast-on.

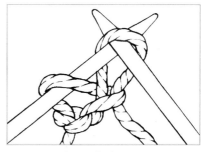

Step 3 Cast on

Step 4 Cast on

BASIC KNIT STITCH

1. Hold the needle with the cast-on stitches in your left hand and hold the empty needle in your right hand. Insert the right needle from front to back into the first stitch on the left needle and wrap the yarn just like in the first step of the cast-on.

2. With the tip of the right needle, pull the wrap through the stitch on the left needle and onto the right needle. Drop the stitch from the left needle. A new stitch is made on the right needle. Repeat steps 1 and 2 until all the stitches from the left needle are on the right needle. Turn the work and hold the needle with the new stitches in your left hand and continue knitting back and forth.

BASIC PURL STITCH

The purl stitch is basically the opposite of the knit stitch. Instead of pulling the wrapped yarn toward you, you push it through the back of the stitch. Because it is harder to see what you are doing, the purl stitch is a bit more difficult to learn than the knit stitch. When you knit one row and then purl one row, you create the stockinette stitch.

Hold the needle with the cast-on stitches in your left hand, and hold the empty needle in your right hand. Insert the right needle from back to front into the first stitch on the left needle and wrap the yarn counterclockwise around the needle as shown. With the tip of the right needle, pull the wrap through the stitch on the left needle and onto the right needle, as in the knit stitch. Drop the stitch from the left needle. A new stitch is made on the right needle. Continue in this way across the row.

Step 1 Basic knit stitch

Step 2 Basic knit stitch

Basic purl stitch

STOCKINETTE STITCH

On straight needles, knit on the right side, purl on the wrong side. On a circular needle, knit every row.

GARTER STITCH

When using straight needles, knit every row. On a circular needle, knit one row, purl one row.

KNIT 2 TOGETHER (K2TOG), OR DECREASE

Hold the needle with the knitted fabric in your left hand and the empty needle in your right hand. Insert the right needle from front to back through the first two stitches on the left needle. Wrap the yarn and pull through the two stitches as if knitting. Drop the two stitches from the left needle. One new stitch is made from two stitches; therefore one stitch is decreased.

INCREASE

The most common way to increase is to knit in the front of the stitch and, without removing the stitch from the left-hand needle, knit in the back of the same stitch, and then drop the stitches from the left needle. This makes two stitches in one stitch.

BIND OFF

Hold the needle with the knitting in your left hand and the empty needle in your right hand. Knit the first two stitches. *With the left needle in front of the right needle, insert the tip of the left needle into the second stitch on the right needle and pull it over the first stitch and off the right needle. One stitch has been bound off. Knit the next stitch; then repeat from the * until all the stitches are bound off.

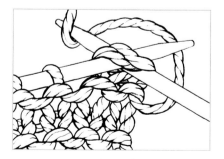

Knit 2 together

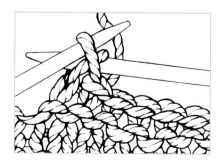

Bind off

big fish, little fish

A MinnowKnits Book

Sporting Life

Sporty, spirited outerwear, perfect for frolicking in autumn leaves or for spring picnics

Cable Guy

This faux-aran pattern is a true QuickKnit, as long as you know how to cable, and the rewards are great—perfect for hard-to-please teenagers.

Bulky Pullover with Cables and Seed Stitch ■ Unisex ■ QuickKnit

SIZES

Child: 4 (6 - 8 - 10) years
Finished chest: 30 (32 - 34 - 36)" / 76 (81 - 86 - 91) cm
Length, shoulder to hem: 15 (16 - 17 - 18)" /
                                    38 (40.5 - 43.5 - 45.5) cm

Adult: small (medium - large)
Finished chest: 44 (48 - 52)" / 112 (122 - 132) cm
Length, shoulder to hem: 26 (26½ - 27)" /
                                    66 (67 - 68.5) cm

MATERIALS

Heavy weight wool that will obtain gauge given below
Child: 515 (610 - 700 - 800) yd. / 465 (550 - 630 - 720) m
Adult: 1340 (1465 - 1600) yd. / 1205 (1320 - 1440) m
Knitting needles size 11 US (0 UK, 8 mm) or size needed to
   obtain gauge
Double pointed needles (dpns) size 11 US (0 UK, 8 mm)
16" / 40 cm circular needle size 11 US (0 UK, 8 mm)
Cable needle (cn)
Stitch holders
Samples in photographs knit in Brown Sheep Lamb's Pride
   Bulky #M06 Deep Charcoal

GAUGE

13 sts and 17 rows = 4" or 10 cm over seed st and cable pat
Always check gauge to save time and ensure correct yardage and correct fit!

Cable Guy | # Child

Seed St

Row 1 (RS): *K1, p1; rep from * to end.
Row 2: K the p sts and p the k sts.
Rep row 2 for seed st.

Cable Pat (over 6 sts)

Row 1 (RS): K6.
Rows 2, 4, 6, 8, and 10: P6.
Row 3: Sl 3 sts to cn and hold to back, k3, k3 from cn.
Rows 5, 7, and 9: Rep row 1.
Rep rows 1–10 for cable pat.

BACK

Cast on 50 (54 - 58 - 62) sts. Work in k1, p1 rib for 1" / 2.5 cm. Work seed st and cable pat as foll: *Row 1 (RS):* Work 8 (10 - 12 - 14) sts seed st, [6 sts cable pat, 8 sts seed st] twice, 6 sts cable pat, work 8 (10 - 12 - 14) sts seed st. Cont in pats as est until piece measures 15 (16 - 17 - 18)" / 38 (40.5 - 43.5 - 45.5) cm from beg or desired length to shoulder. Work 14 (16 - 17 - 19) sts and place on a holder for one shoulder, bind off next 22 (22 - 24 - 24) sts for back neck, work rem sts, and place on a 2nd holder for other shoulder.

FRONT

Work as for back until piece measures 13 (14 - 15 - 16)" / 33 (35.5 - 38.5 - 40.5) cm from beg or 2" / 5 cm less than length of back; end with a WS row. **Shape neck:** *Next row (RS):* Work 18 (20 - 21 - 23) sts, join 2nd ball of yarn, and bind off center 14 (14 - 16 - 16) sts; work to end. Working both sides at same time, bind off from each neck edge 2 sts twice—14 (16 - 17 - 19) sts rem on each side. Work even until front is same length as back. Place rem sts on holders.

SHOULDER SEAMS

For each shoulder, k seam tog as foll: Sl front and back shoulder sts from holders to 2 dpns. Hold pieces together with *wrong sides facing* each other and sweater front facing you. With a 3rd dpn, k first st from front needle tog with first st from back needle, *k next st from front and back needles tog, sl first st over 2nd st to bind off; rep from * until all sts are bound off. Cut yarn and pull end through loop.

SLEEVES

Mark for sleeves 7 (7½ - 8 - 8½)" / 17.5 (19 - 20.5 - 21.5) cm down from shoulder seam on front and back. With RS facing and larger needles, pick up and k46 (48 - 52 - 56) sts between markers. Work in seed st and cable pat as foll: Work 6 (7 - 9 - 11) sts seed st, [6 sts cable pat, 8 sts seed st] twice, 6 sts cable pat, work 6 (7 - 9 - 11) sts seed st. Cont in pats as est for 2 more rows. Working dec sts into pat, dec 1 st each end on next row, then every 4th row 7 (10 - 12 - 14) times more, every 2nd row 3 (1 - 0 - 0) times—24 (24 - 26 - 26) sts rem. Work even until sleeve measures 10 (12 - 13½ - 15)" / 25.5 (30.5 - 34 - 38) cm or desired length. Work in k1, p1 rib for 1" / 2.5 cm. Bind off loosely and evenly in rib.

FINISHING

Sew side and sleeve seams. **Neckband:** With RS facing and circular needle, pick up and k54 (54 - 58 - 58) sts evenly around neck edge. Join and work in k1, p1 rib for 1" / 2.5 cm. Bind off in pat.

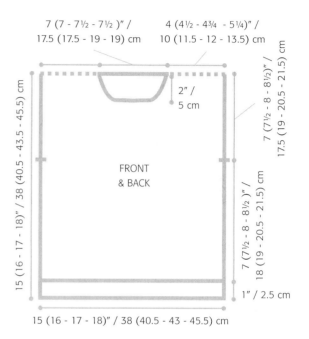

7 (7 - 7½ - 7½)" / 17.5 (17.5 - 19 - 19) cm

4 (4½ - 4¾ - 5¼)" / 10 (11.5 - 12 - 13.5) cm

7 (7½ - 8 - 8½)" / 17.5 (19 - 20.5 - 21.5) cm

2" / 5 cm

FRONT & BACK

15 (16 - 17 - 18)" / 38 (40.5 - 43.5 - 45.5) cm

7 (7½ - 8 - 8½)" / 18 (19 - 20.5 - 21.5) cm

1" / 2.5 cm

15 (16 - 17 - 18)" / 38 (40.5 - 43 - 45.5) cm

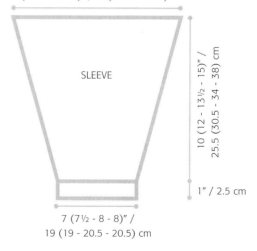

14 (15 - 16 - 17)" / 35 (38 - 41 - 43) cm

SLEEVE

10 (12 - 13½ - 15)" / 25.5 (30.5 - 34 - 38) cm

1" / 2.5 cm

7 (7½ - 8 - 8)" / 19 (19 - 20.5 - 20.5) cm

Cable Guy | Adult

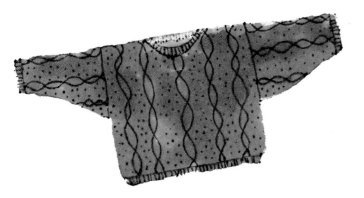

Seed St

Row 1 (RS): *K1, p1; rep from * to end.
Row 2: K the p sts and p the k sts.
Rep row 2 for seed st.

Cable Pat (over 6 sts)

Row 1 (RS): K6.
Rows 2, 4, 6, 8, and 10: P6.
Row 3: Sl 3 sts to cn and hold to back, k3,
    k3 from cn.
Rows 5, 7, and 9: Rep row 1.
Rep rows 1–10 for cable pat.

BACK

Cast on 72 (78 - 84) sts. Work in k1, p1 rib for 2" / 5 cm. Work seed st and cable pat as foll: *Row 1 (RS):* Work 5 (8 - 9) sts seed st, [6 sts cable pat, 8 (8 - 9) sts seed st] 4 times, 6 sts cable pat, work 5 (8 - 9) sts seed st. Cont in pats as est until piece measures 26 (26½ - 27)" / 66 (67 - 68.5) cm from beg or desired length to shoulder. Work 23 (26 - 28) sts and place on a holder for one shoulder, bind off next 26 (26 - 28) sts for back neck, work rem sts, and place on a 2nd holder for other shoulder.

FRONT

Work as for back until piece measures 23 (23½ - 24)" / 58.5 (59.5 - 61) cm from beg or 3" / 7.5 cm less than length of back; end with a WS row. **Shape neck:** *Next row (RS):* Work 29 (32 - 34) sts, join 2nd ball of yarn, and bind off center 14 (14 - 16) sts; work to end. Working both sides at same time, bind off from each neck edge 2 sts twice, 1 st twice—23 (26 - 28) sts rem each side. Work even until front is same length as back. Place rem sts on holders.

SHOULDER SEAMS

For each shoulder, k seam tog as foll: Sl front and back shoulder sts from holders to 2 dpns. Hold pieces together with *wrong sides facing* each other and sweater front facing you. With a

3rd dpn, k first st from front needle tog with first st from back needle, *k next st from front and back needles tog, sl first st over 2nd st to bind off; rep from * until all sts are bound off. Cut yarn and pull end through loop.

SLEEVES

Mark for sleeves 10 (10½ - 11)″ / 25.5 (26.5 - 28) cm down from shoulder seam on front and back. With RS facing and larger needles, pick up and k66 (68 - 71) sts between markers. Work in seed st and cable pat as foll: Work 9 (10 - 10) sts seed st, [6 sts cable pat, 8 (8 - 9) sts seed st] 3 times, 6 sts cable pat, work 9 (10 - 10) sts seed st. Cont in pats as est for 4 more rows. Working dec sts into pat, dec 1 st each end on next row, then every 6th row 3 (2 - 1) times more, every 4th row 13 (15 - 17) times—32 (32 - 33) sts rem. Work even until sleeve measures 19 (19½ - 20)″ / 48 (49.5 - 50.5) cm or 2″ / 5 cm less than desired length. Work in k1, p1 rib for 2″ / 5 cm. Bind off loosely and evenly in rib.

FINISHING

Sew side and sleeve seams. **Neckband:** With RS facing and circular needle, pick up and k66 (66 - 70) sts evenly around neck edge. Join and work in k1, p1 rib for 1″ / 2.5 cm. Bind off in pat.

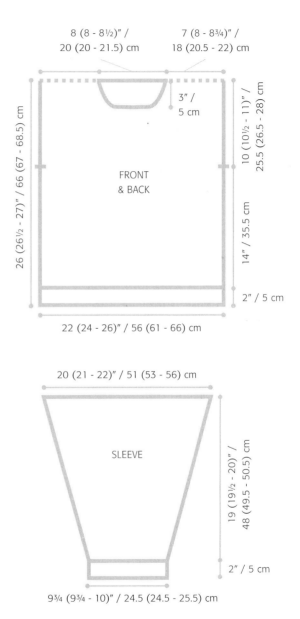

Garter Cardi

So many knitters asked for this pattern that I had to include it in this sized-up collection. Very simple to knit, with garter stitch trim, Garter Cardi is perfect for beginners or those returning to knitting. The spiral Fimo buttons really give this little sweater zip!

Worsted Weight Cropped Cardigan with Garter Stitch Trim
Women's/Girl's ■ QuickKnit

SIZES

Child: 2 (4 - 6 - 8) years
Finished chest: 25 (28 - 31 - 34)" /
        63 (70 - 78 - 85) cm
Length, shoulder to hem: 12 (14 - 15 - 16)" /
        30 (35 - 37.5 - 40) cm

Adult: small (medium - large)
Finished chest: 40 (44 - 48)" /
        101.5 (112 - 122) cm
Length, shoulder to hem: 17 (17½ - 18)" /
        43 (44.5 - 45.5) cm

MATERIALS

Worsted weight yarn that will obtain gauge given below
Child: 320 (410 - 520 - 630) yd. / 290 (370 - 470 - 570) m
Adult: 1275 (1400 - 1525) yd. / 1150 (1260 - 1370) m
Knitting needles size 8 US (6 UK, 5 mm) or size needed to obtain gauge
Double pointed needles (dpns) size 8 US (6 UK, 5 mm)
Stitch holders
Child: 3 (3 - 3 - 4) ¾" / 2 cm buttons
Adult: Four ¾" / 2 cm buttons
Samples knit in Manos del Uruguay #48 Cherry for child; #63 Heliotrope
*   for adult*

GAUGE

18 sts and 24 rows = 4" / 10 cm in St st
Always check gauge to save time and ensure correct yardage and fit!

Garter Cardi | Child

BACK

Cast on 57 (63 - 70 - 77) sts. Work in garter st (k all rows) for 3″ / 7.5 cm; end with a WS row. *Next row (RS):* K. Cont in St st until piece measures 12 (14 - 15 - 16)″ / 30.5 (35.5 - 38 - 40.5) cm or desired length to shoulder. Work 17 (20 - 23 - 25) sts and place on holder for one shoulder, bind off 23 (23 - 24 - 27) sts for neck, work rem sts, and place on separate holder for other shoulder.

LEFT FRONT

Cast on 32 (35 - 39 - 42) sts. Work in garter st for 3″ / 7.5 cm, end with a WS row. *Next row (RS):* K. *Next row:* K6, p rem sts. Rep last 2 rows until piece measures 10 (12 - 13 - 14)″ / 25.5 (30.5 - 33 - 35.5) cm or 2″ / 5 cm less than length of back; end with a WS row. **Shape neck:** *Next row (RS):* K to last 6 sts; sl rem 6 sts to holder. *Next row:* Bind off 3 sts, p to end. Cont to bind off at the beg of every WS row 3 sts 0 (0 - 1 - 1) times more, 2 sts twice, 1 st 2 (2 - 0 - 1) times—17 (20 - 23 - 25) sts rem. Work even until front measures same

length as back. Place sts on holder. Place markers on front band for 3 (3 - 3 - 4) buttons, first one ¾″ / 2 cm above the garter stitch edging, last one ¼″ / .5 cm below neck shaping, and 1 (1 - 1 - 2) others spaced evenly between.

RIGHT FRONT

Work as for left front for 3″ / 7.5 cm, end WS row. *Next row (RS):* K. *Next row:* P to last 6 sts, k6. Rep last 2 rows, working a buttonhole row opposite each marker on RS rows as foll: K2, k2tog, yo, k2, k rem sts. Work until piece measures same as left front to neck; end with a RS row. **Shape neck:** *Next row (WS):* P to last 6 sts, sl rem 6 sts to holder. *Next row:* Bind off 3 sts, k to end. Cont to work neck, shaping beg of RS rows as for left front. Work even until same length as back. Sl rem sts to holder.

SHOULDER SEAMS

For each shoulder, k seam tog as foll: Sl front and back shoulder sts from holders to 2 dpns. Hold pieces together with wrong sides facing each other and sweater front facing you. With a 3rd dpn, k first st from front needle tog with first st from back needle, *k next st from front and back needles tog, sl first st over 2nd st to bind off; rep from * until all sts are bound off. Cut yarn and pull end through loop.

SLEEVES

Place markers on front and back for armholes 6½ (7 - 7½ - 8)″ / 16.5 (17.5 - 19 - 21) cm down from shoulder seams. With RS facing, pick up and k58 (64 - 68 - 72) sts between

markers. Starting with a p row, work 5 rows
St st. Dec 1 st each edge next row, then every
4th row 4 (1 - 1 - 1) times more, then every
2nd row 6 (12 - 13 - 15) times—36 (36 - 38 -
38) sts rem. Work even until sleeve measures 6
(7 - 8 - 9)″ / 15 (17.5 - 20 - 22.5) cm or 2″ / 5
cm less than desired length. Work in garter st
for 2″ / 5 cm. Bind off evenly knitwise.

FINISHING

Neckband: With RS facing, beg at right front
neck, k6 sts from holder, pick up and k11 (11 -
13 - 13) sts along right neck edge, 23 (23 -
24 - 27) sts across back neck, 11 (11 - 13 - 13)
sts along left neck edge, k6 sts from left front
holder—57 (57 - 62 - 65) sts. Work in garter st
for ¾″ / 2 cm. Bind off knitwise. Sew side and
sleeve seams. Sew on buttons.

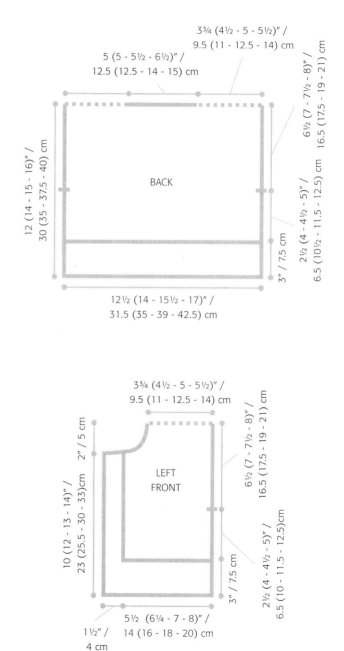

3¾ (4½ - 5 - 5½)″ /
9.5 (11 - 12.5 - 14) cm

5 (5 - 5½ - 6½)″ /
12.5 (12.5 - 14 - 15) cm

6½ (7 - 7½ - 8)″ /
16.5 (17.5 - 19 - 21) cm

BACK

12 (14 - 15 - 16)″ /
30 (35 - 37.5 - 40) cm

3″ / 7.5 cm

2½ (4 - 4½ - 5)″ /
6.5 (10½ - 11.5 - 12.5) cm

12½ (14 - 15½ - 17)″ /
31.5 (35 - 39 - 42.5) cm

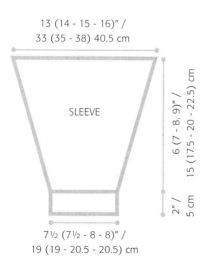

13 (14 - 15 - 16)″ /
33 (35 - 38) 40.5 cm

SLEEVE

6 (7 - 8. 9)″ /
15 (17.5 - 20 - 22.5) cm

2″ /
5 cm

7½ (7½ - 8 - 8)″ /
19 (19 - 20.5 - 20.5) cm

3¾ (4½ - 5 - 5½)″ /
9.5 (11 - 12.5 - 14) cm

6½ (7 - 7½ - 8)″ /
16.5 (17.5 - 19 - 21) cm

2″ / 5 cm

LEFT
FRONT

10 (12 - 13 - 14)″ /
23 (25.5 - 30 - 33)cm

3″ / 7.5 cm

2½ (4 - 4½ - 5)″ /
6.5 (10 - 11.5 - 12.5)cm

5½ (6¼ - 7 - 8)″ /
14 (16 - 18 - 20) cm

1½″ /
4 cm

Garter Cardi | Adult

BACK

Cast on 92 (101 - 110) sts. Work in garter st (k all rows) for 3½" / 9 cm, end with a WS row. *Next row (RS):* K. Cont in St st until piece measures 17 (17½ - 18)" / 43 (44.5 - 45.5) cm or desired length to shoulder. Work 30 (34 - 37) sts and place on holder for one shoulder, bind off 32 (33 - 36) sts for neck, work rem sts, and place on separate holder for other shoulder.

LEFT FRONT

Cast on 50 (55 - 59) sts. Work in garter st for 3½" / 9 cm, end with a WS row. *Next row (RS):* K. *Next row:* K9, p rem sts. Rep last 2 rows until piece measures 14 (14½ - 15)" / 35.5 (37 - 38) cm or 3" / 7.5 cm less than length of back, end with a WS row. **Shape neck:** *Next row (RS):* K to last 9 sts, sl rem 9 sts to holder. *Next row:* Bind off 3 sts, p to end. Cont to bind off at beg of every WS row 3 sts once more, 2 sts 2 (2 - 3) times, 1 st 1 (2 - 1) time—30 (34 - 37) sts rem. Work even until

front measures same length as back. Place sts on holder. Place markers on front band for 4 buttons, first one just above garter stitch edging, last one ¼" / .5 cm below neck shaping, and other 2 spaced evenly between.

RIGHT FRONT

Work as for left front for 3½" / 9 cm, end with a WS row. *Next row (RS):* K. *Next row:* P to last 9 sts and k9. Rep last 2 rows, working a buttonhole row opposite each marker on RS rows as foll: K3, k2tog, yo, k2, k rem sts. Work until piece measures 14 (14½ - 15)" / 35.5 (37 - 38) cm; end with a RS row. **Shape neck:** *Next row (WS):* P to last 9 sts; sl rem 9 sts to holder. *Next row:* Bind off 3 sts, k to end. Cont to work neck, shaping beg of RS rows as for left front. Work even until same length as back. Sl rem sts to holder.

SHOULDER SEAMS

For each shoulder, k seam tog as foll: Sl front and back shoulder sts from holders to 2 dpns. Hold pieces together with wrong sides facing each other and sweater front facing you. With a 3rd dpn, k first st from front needle tog with first st from back needle, *k next st from front and back needles tog, sl first st over 2nd st to bind off; rep from * until all sts are bound off. Cut yarn and pull end through loop.

SLEEVES

Place markers on front and back for armholes 8½ (9 - 9½)" / 21.5 (23 - 24) cm down from shoulder seams. With RS facing, pick up and k78 (82 - 88) sts between markers. Starting with a p row, work 3 rows St st. Dec 1 st each edge next row, then every 6th row 7 (5 - 0) times more, then every 4th row 11 (14 - 22) times—40 (42 - 42) sts rem. Work even until sleeve measures 15½" / 39.5 cm, or 2½" / 6.5 cm less than desired length. Work in garter st for 2½" / 6.5 cm. Bind off evenly knitwise.

FINISHING

Neckband: With RS facing, beg at right front neck, k9 sts from holder, pick up and k60 (62 - 68) sts around neck including sts from back holder, k9 sts from left front holder—78 (80 - 86) sts. K 2 rows. Bind off knitwise. Sew side and sleeve seams. Sew on buttons.

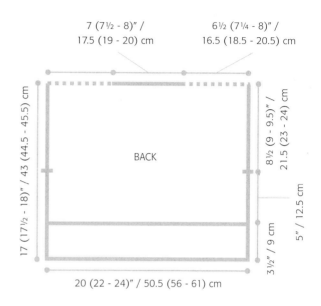

7 (7½ - 8)" / 17.5 (19 - 20) cm

6½ (7¼ - 8)" / 16.5 (18.5 - 20.5) cm

BACK

17 (17½ - 18)" / 43 (44.5 - 45.5) cm

8½ (9 - 9.5)" / 21.5 (23 - 24) cm

5" / 12.5 cm

3½" / 9 cm

20 (22 - 24)" / 50.5 (56 - 61) cm

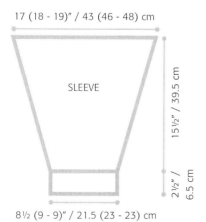

17 (18 - 19)" / 43 (46 - 48) cm

SLEEVE

15½" / 39.5 cm

2½" / 6.5 cm

8½ (9 - 9)" / 21.5 (23 - 23) cm

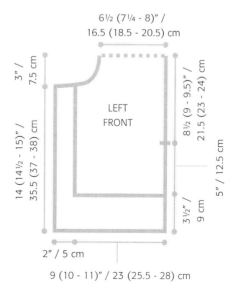

6½ (7¼ - 8)" / 16.5 (18.5 - 20.5) cm

3" / 7.5 cm

LEFT FRONT

8½ (9 - 9.5)" / 21.5 (23 - 24) cm

14 (14½ - 15)" / 35.5 (37 - 38) cm

5" / 12.5 cm

3½" / 9 cm

2" / 5 cm

9 (10 - 11)" / 23 (25.5 - 28) cm

Striper

Cropped and swingy, this cotton pullover is easy to knit and easy to wear. This sweater has cabled detailing in the wide stand-up collar and down the center of the sleeve.

SIZES

Child: 2 (4 - 6 - 8) years
Finished chest: 28 (30 - 32 - 34)" /
            71 (76 - 81 - 86) cm
Length, shoulder to hem: 12 (13 - 14 - 15)" /
            30 (33 - 35 - 38) cm

Adult: small (medium - large)
Finished chest: 48 (52 - 56)" / 122 (132 - 142) cm
Length, shoulder to hem: 19 (20 - 21)" /
            48 (51 - 53) cm

MATERIALS

Aran weight yarn that will obtain gauge given below
Child: 205 (250 - 295 - 370) yd. / 185 (225 - 265 - 335) m in yellow (MC)
165 (200 - 235 - 295) yd. / 150 (180 - 210 - 265) m in white (CC)
Adult: 600 (660 - 730) yd. / 540 (600 - 660) m in magenta (MC)
480 (525 - 580) yd. / 430 (475 - 520) m in yellow (CC)
Knitting needles sizes 7 and 8 US (7 and 6 UK, 4.5 and 5 mm) or size needed
    to obtain gauge
Double pointed needles (dpns) size 8 US (6 UK, 5 mm)
Circular needle size 8 US (6 UK, 5 mm), 16" / 40 cm long
Cable needle (cn)
Stitch holders
Samples in photographs knit in Crystal Palace Monterey #04 Yellow and #57
    White for child; #048 Magenta and #04 Yellow for adult

GAUGE

16 sts and 24 rows = 4" or 10 cm in St st
Always check gauge to save time and ensure correct yardage and correct fit!

Striper | Child

Stripe Pat

*Work 8 (8 - 8 - 10) rows MC, 8 (8 - 8 - 10) rows CC; rep from * for stripe pat.

Cable Pat #1 (over 10 sts)

Note: When changing color in stripe pat, work first row of new color (WS): P10.

Rows 1, 3, 5, and 7 (WS): K2, p6, k2.

Rows 2, 6, and 8: P2, k6, p2.

Row 4: P2, sl 3 sts to cn and hold to back, k3, k3 from cn, p2.

Rep rows 1–8 for cable pat #1.

Cable Pat #2 (multiple of 8 sts, worked in the round)

Rnds 1, 2, and 4: *K2, p1, k4, p1; rep from * around.

Rnd 3: *K2, p1, sl 2 sts to cn and hold to back, k2, k2 from cn, p1.

Rep rnds 1–4 for cable pat #2.

BACK

With smaller needles and MC, cast on 56 (60 - 64 - 68) sts. Work stripe pat as foll: Work first 2 rows in MC and k1, p1 rib; then change to larger needles and cont in MC and St st for 6 (6 - 6 - 8) more rows. Cont in stripe pat until piece measures 12 (13 - 14 - 15)" / 30 (33 - 35 - 38) cm from beg or desired length to shoulder. Work 16 (17 - 19 - 20) sts and place on a holder for one shoulder; bind off next 24 (26 - 26 - 28) sts for back neck, work rem sts, and place on a 2nd holder for other shoulder.

FRONT

Work as for back until piece measures 10 (11 - 12 - 13)" / 25 (27.5 - 30 - 32.5) cm from beg or 2" / 5 cm less than length of back; end with WS row. **Shape neck:** *Next row (RS):* K22 (23 - 25 - 26) sts, join 2nd ball of yarn and bind off center 12 (14 - 14 - 16) sts; k to end. Working both sides at same time, bind off from each neck edge 2 sts twice, 1 st twice—16 (17 - 19 - 20) sts rem each side. Work even until same length as back. Place rem sts on holders.

SHOULDER SEAMS

For each shoulder, k seam tog as foll: Sl front and back shoulder sts from holders to 2 dpns. Hold pieces together with wrong sides facing each other and sweater front facing you. With a 3rd dpn, k first st from front needle tog with first st from back needle, *k next st from front and back needles tog, sl first st over 2nd st to bind off; rep from * until all sts are bound off. Cut yarn and pull end through loop.

SLEEVES

Mark for sleeves 5½ (6 - 6½ - 7)" / 13.5 (15 - 16.5 - 17.5) cm down from shoulder seam on front and back. With larger needles, RS facing and MC (CC - MC - CC), pick up and k48 (52 - 56 - 60) sts between markers. Work sleeve shaping as foll: Work 4 rows even, then dec 1 st each end on next row, then every 6th row 2 (6 - 7 - 9) times more, every 4th row 6 (3 - 4 - 3) times—30 (32 - 32 - 34) sts rem. *At the same time*, starting with row 1 of stripe pat and cable pat #1, work as foll: Work 19 (21 - 23 - 25) sts in St st, 10 sts cable pat #1, 19 (21 - 23 - 25) sts in St st. Cont in pats as est, working dec as indicated; then work even until sleeve measures 8 (10 - 11½ - 13)" / 20.5 (25.5 - 29 - 33) cm or desired length; end with 8 rows CC (8 rows CC - 2 rows MC - 4 rows MC). Change to smaller needles, and with MC work in k1, p1 rib for 4 rows. Bind off loosely and evenly in rib.

FINISHING

Sew side and sleeve seams. **Neckband:** With RS facing, circular needle and MC, pick up and k64 (64 - 64 - 72) sts evenly around neck edge. Join and work in cable pat #2 for 1½" / 4 cm. Bind off in pat.

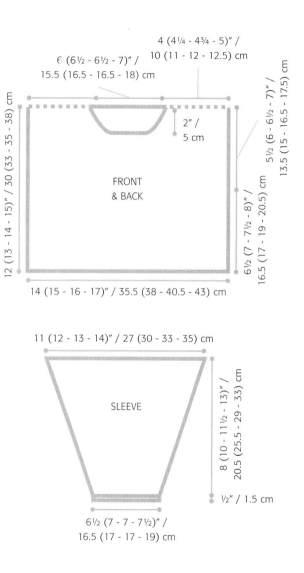

Striper | Adult

BACK

With smaller needles and MC, cast on 96 (104 - 112) sts. Work stripe pat as foll: Work first 2 rows in MC and k1, p1 rib; then, with larger needles, cont in MC and St st for 8 more rows. Cont in stripe pat until piece measures 19 (20 - 21)″ / 48 (51 - 53) cm from beg or desired length to shoulder. Work 30 (34 - 38) sts and place on a holder for one shoulder, bind off next 36 sts for back neck, work rem sts, and place on a 2nd holder for other shoulder.

FRONT

Work as for back until piece measures 16 (17 - 18)″ / 40.5 (43.5 - 45.5) cm from beg or 3″ / 7.5 cm less than length of back; end with WS row. **Shape neck:** *Next row (RS):* K38 (42 - 46) sts, join 2nd ball of yarn and bind off center 20 sts, k to end. Working both sides at same time, bind off from each neck edge 2 sts twice, 1 st 4 times—30 (34 - 38) sts rem each side. Work even until same length as back. Place rem sts on holders.

SHOULDER SEAMS

For each shoulder, k seam tog as foll: Sl front and back shoulder sts from holders to 2 dpns. Hold pieces together with wrong sides facing each other and sweater front facing you. With a 3rd dpn, k first st from front needle tog with

---

Stripe Pat

*Work 10 rows MC, 10 rows CC; rep from * for stripe pat.

Cable Pat #1 (over 10 sts)

Note: When changing color in stripe pat, work first row of new color (WS): P10.
Rows 1, 3, 5, and 7 (WS): K2, p6, k2.
Rows 2, 6, and 8: P2, k6, p2.
Row 4: P2, sl 3 sts to cn and hold to back, k3, k3 from cn, p2.
Rep rows 1–8 for cable pat #1.

Cable Pat #2 (multiple of 9 sts, worked in the round)

Rnds 1, 2, and 4: *K3, p1, k4, p1; rep from * around.
Rnd 3: *K3, p1, sl 2 sts to cn and hold to back, k2, k2 from cn, p1.
Rep rnds 1–4 for cable pat #2.

first st from back needle, *k next st from front and back needles tog, sl first st over 2nd st to bind off; rep from * until all sts are bound off. Cut yarn and pull end through loop.

SLEEVES

Mark for sleeves 9½ (10 - 10½)″ / 24 (25.5 - 26.5) cm down from shoulder seam on front and back. With larger needles, RS facing and CC, pick up and k80 (84 - 88) sts between markers. Work sleeve shaping as foll: Work 4 rows even, then dec 1 st each end on next row, then every 4th row 20 (20 - 19) times more, every 6th (2nd - 2nd) row 1 (3 - 5) times—36 (36 - 38) sts rem. *At the same time*, starting with row 1 of stripe pat and cable pat #1, work as foll: Work 35 (37 - 39) sts in St st, 10 sts cable pat #1, 35 (37 - 39) sts in St st. Cont in pats as est, working dec as indicated, then work even until sleeve measures 16″ / 40.5 cm or desired length, end with 6 rows MC. Change to smaller needles, and with MC work in k1, p1 rib for 4 rows. Bind off loosely and evenly in rib.

FINISHING

Sew side and sleeve seams. **Neckband:** With RS facing, circular needle and MC, pick up and k108 sts evenly around neck edge. Join and work in cable pat #2 for 1½″ / 4 cm. Bind off in pat.

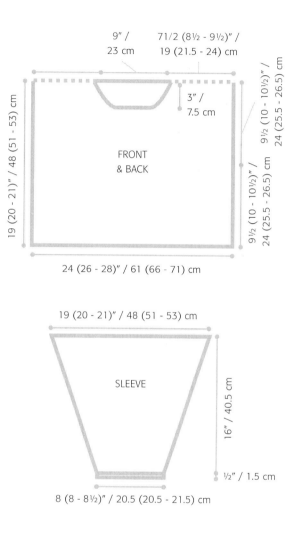

Get Fleeced

Everyone wants a fleece vest, and here's one you can knit in a snap! A perfect beginner project, this vest is great on everyone from toddlers to teens and even adults. The silhouette is fashioned to be cozy and comfortable, and it is a true QuickKnit at three stitches to the inch.

Bulk Vest with Zipper and Collar ▪ Unisex ▪ QuickKnit

SIZES

Child: 4 (6 - 8 - 10) years
Finished chest (closed): 30 (32 - 34 - 36)″ /
                   76 (81.5 - 86 - 91.5) cm
Length, shoulder to hem: 16 (16 - 18 - 18)″ /
                   40 (40 - 46 - 46) cm

Adult: small (medium - large)
Finished chest (closed): 40 (44 - 48)″ /
                   101 (112 - 122) cm
Length, shoulder to hem: 25 (25 - 27)″ /
                   63.5 (63.5 - 68.5) cm

MATERIALS

Bulky weight wool that will obtain gauge given below
Child: 240 (275 - 310 - 350) yd. / 215 (250 - 280 - 315) m
Adult: 535 (610 - 690) yd. / 500 (550 - 620) m
Knitting needles size 10½ US (3 UK, 6.5 mm) or size needed to obtain gauge
Double pointed needles (dpns) size 10½ US (3 UK, 6.5 mm)
Child: 6 (16 - 18 - 18)″ / 40 (40 - 46 - 46) cm separating zipper
Adult: 24 (24 - 26)″ / 61 (61 - 66) cm separating zipper
Stitch holders
Samples in photographs knit in Rowan Chunky Soft #150

GAUGE

12 sts and 18 rows = 4″ / 10 cm in St st
Always check gauge to save time and ensure correct yardage and correct fit!

Note: K first and last st of every row for garter st selvage

Get Fleeced | Child

BACK

Cast on 46 (49 - 52 - 55) sts. Work in St st with garter st selvage each edge (see note on page 21) for 9½ (9½ - 10½ - 10½)" / 24 (24 - 27 - 27) cm or desired length to armhole, end with a WS row. **Shape armhole:** Bind off 3 sts beg of next 2 rows. *Next row (RS):* K1, sl 1, k1, psso, k to last 3 sts, k2tog, k1. *Next row:* K1, p to last st, k1. Rep last 2 rows a total of 3 times—34 (37 - 40 - 43) sts. Work even, keeping garter st selvage each edge, until armhole measures 6½ (6½ - 7½ - 7½)" / 16 (16 - 19 - 19) cm. Work 8 (9 - 10 - 11) sts and place on a holder for one shoulder, bind off next 18 (19 - 20 - 21) sts for back neck, work rem sts, and place on a 2nd holder for other shoulder.

LEFT FRONT

Cast on 23 (25 - 26 - 28) sts. Work in St st with garter st selvage each edge until piece measures same length as back to armhole; end with a WS row. **Shape armhole:** *Next row (RS):* Bind off 3 sts, k rem sts. *Next row:* K1, p to last st, k1. *Next row:* K1, sl 1, k1, psso, k rem sts. Rep last 2 rows a total of 3 times—17 (19 - 20) sts rem. Work even, keeping garter st selvage each edge, until armhole measures 4½ (4½ - 5½ - 5½)" / 11.5 (11.5 - 14 - 14) cm; end with a RS row. **Shape neck:** *Next row (WS):* Bind off 4 (5 - 5 - 5) sts, p to last st, k1. Keeping selvage st at armhole edge, cont to bind off at beg of WS rows 2 sts 2 (2 - 2 - 3) times, dec 1 st every other row 1 (1 - 1 - 0) time—8 (9 - 10 - 11) sts rem. Work even until same length as back. Place sts on holder.

RIGHT FRONT

Work same as left front to armhole; end RS row. **Shape armhole:** *Next row (WS):* Bind off 3 sts, p to last st, k1. *Next row:* K to last 3 sts, k2tog, k1. *Next row:* K1, p to last st, k1. Rep last 2 rows a total of 3 times—17 (19 - 20) sts rem. Work even until piece measures same as left front to neck, end with a WS row. **Shape**

neck: *Next row (RS):* Bind off 4 (5 - 5 - 5) sts, k rem sts. Cont to work neck shaping at beg of RS rows as for left front, and keep selvage st at armhole edge. Work even until piece measures same as back. Place sts on holder.

SHOULDER SEAMS

For each shoulder, k seam tog as foll: Sl front and back shoulder sts from holders to 2 dpns. Hold pieces together with the wrong sides facing each other and sweater front facing you. With a 3rd dpn, k first st from front needle tog with first st from back needle, *k next st from front and back needles tog, sl first st over 2nd st to bind off; rep from * until all sts are bound off. Cut yarn and pull end through loop.

FINISHING

Sew side seams. **Neckband:** With RS facing, pick up and k47 (49 - 51 - 53) sts evenly around neck edge. Work in St st with 1 garter st each edge for 2" / 5 cm. Bind off. Sew in zipper inside of garter st selvage.

6 (6¼ - 6½ - 7)" /
15 (16 - 16.5 - 17.5) cm

2¾ (3 - 3½ - 3¾)" /
7 (7.5 - 9 - 9.5) cm

6½ (6½ - 7½ - 7½)" /
16 (16 - 19 - 19) cm

16 (16 - 18 - 18)" /
40 (40 - 46 - 46) cm

BACK

9½ (9½ - 10½ - 10½)" /
24 (24 - 27 - 27) cm

15 (16 - 17 - 18)" /
38 (40.5 - 43 - 45.5) cm

2¾ (3 - 3½ - 3¾)" /
7 (7.5 - 9 - 9.5) cm

2" / 5 cm

6½ (6½ - 7½ - 7½)" /
16 (16 - 19 - 19) cm

14 (14 - 16 - 16)" /
35 (35 - 41 - 41) cm

LEFT
FRONT

9½ (9½ - 10½ - 10½)" /
24 (24 - 27 - 27) cm

7½ (8 - 8½ - 9)" /
19 (20.5 - 21.5 - 23) cm

Get Fleeced | Adult

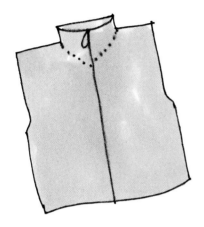

BACK

Cast on 62 (68 - 74) sts. Work in St st with garter st selvage each edge (see note on page 21), for 15 (15 - 16)″ / 38 (38 - 40.5) cm or desired length to armhole, end with a WS row. **Shape armhole:** Bind off 2 (2 - 3) sts at beg of next 2 rows. *Next row (RS):* K1, sl 1, k1, psso, k to last 3 sts, k2tog, k1. *Next row:* K1, p to last st, k1. Rep last 2 rows a total of 4 times— 50 (56 - 60) sts. Work even, keeping garter st selvage each edge, until armhole measures 10 (10 - 11)″ / 25.5 (25.5 - 28) cm. Work 13 (16 - 17) sts and place on a holder for one shoulder, bind off next 24 (24 - 26) sts for back neck, work rem sts, and place on a 2nd holder for other shoulder.

LEFT FRONT

Cast on 32 (35 - 38) sts. Work in St st with garter st selvage each edge until piece measures same as back to armhole; end with a WS row. **Shape armhole:** *Next row (RS):* Bind off 2 (2 - 3) sts, k rem sts. *Next row:* K1, p to last st, k1. *Next row:* K1, sl 1, k1, psso, k rem sts. Rep last 2 rows a total of 4 times—26 (29 - 31) sts rem. Work even, keeping garter st selvage each edge until armhole measures 7 (7 - 8)″ / 18 (18 - 20.5) cm; end with a RS row. **Shape neck:** *Next row (WS):* Bind off 4 (4 - 5) sts, p to last st, k1. Keeping selvage st at armhole edge, cont to bind off at beg of WS rows 3 sts once, 2 sts twice, dec 1 st every other row twice—13 (16 - 17) sts rem. Work even until same length as back. Place sts on holder.

RIGHT FRONT

Work same as left front to armhole; end RS row. **Shape armhole:** *Next row (WS):* Bind off 2 (2 - 3) sts, p to last st, k1. *Next row:* K to last 3 sts, k2tog, k1. Next row: K1, p to last st, k1. Rep last 2 rows a total of 4 times—26 (29 - 31) sts rem. Work even until piece measures same as left front to neck; end with a WS row. **Shape neck:** *Next row (RS):* Bind off 4

(4 - 5) sts, k to end. Cont to work neck shaping beg of RS rows as for left front and keep selvage st at armhole edge. Work even until same length as back. Place sts on holder.

SHOULDER SEAMS

For each shoulder, k seam tog as foll: Sl front and back shoulder sts from holders to 2 dpns. Hold pieces together with the wrong sides facing each other and sweater front facing you. With a 3rd dpn, k first st from front needle tog with first st from back needle, *k next st from front and back needles tog, sl first st over 2nd st to bind off; rep from * until all sts are bound off. Cut yarn and pull end through loop.

FINISHING

Sew side seams. **Neckband:** With RS facing, pick up and k54 (54 - 58) sts evenly around neck edge. Work in St st with 1 garter st each edge for 3″ / 7.5 cm. Bind off. Sew in zipper inside of garter st selvage.

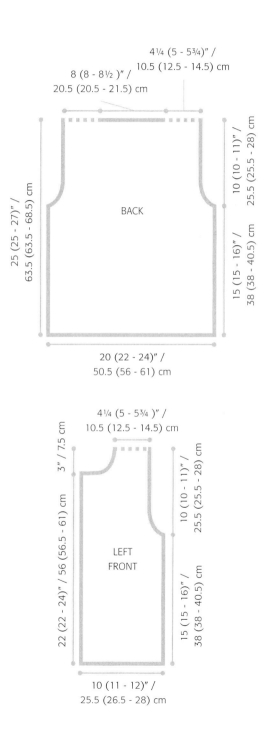

Garter-T

Cropped, with a wide stand-up collar, this garter stitch delight is a speedster. Make very sure you get your gauge, however; bulky cotton does not look neatly knit in garter stitch if the gauge is too loose.

Bulky Garter Stitch Pullover ▪ Women's/Girl's ▪ QuickKnit

SIZES

Child: 2 (4 - 6 - 8) years
Finished chest: 26 (28 - 30 - 32)" /
           66 (71 - 76 - 81) cm
Length, shoulder to hem: 12 (13 - 14 - 15)" /
           30 (33 - 35 - 38) cm

Adult: small (medium - large)
Finished chest: 40 (44 - 48)" /
           101 (112 - 122) cm
Length, shoulder to hem: 18 (18½ - 19)" /
           30 (33 - 35 - 38) cm

MATERIALS

Bulky weight yarn that will obtain gauge given below
Child: 320 (375 - 430 - 495) yd. / 290 (340 - 390 - 445) m
Adult: 750 (850 - 950) yd. / 675 (765 - 855) m
Knitting needles size 10½ US (3 UK, 6.5 mm) or size needed to obtain gauge
Double pointed needles (dpns) 10½ US (3 UK, 6.5 mm)
16" / 40 cm circular needle 10½ US (3 UK, 6.5 mm)
Stitch holders
Samples in photographs knit in Berroco Pronto #4409 Lolita Lime

GAUGE

14 sts and 26 rows = 4" or 10 cm over garter st
Always check gauge to save time and ensure correct yardage and correct fit!

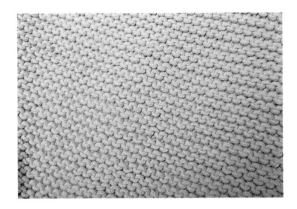

Garter-T | Child

BACK

With straight needles, cast on 47 (51 - 54 - 58) sts. Work garter st (k every row) for 12 (13 - 14 - 15)″ / 30 (33 - 35 - 38) cm or desired length to shoulder. Work 15 (16 - 17 - 18) sts and place on a holder for one shoulder, bind off next 17 (19 - 20 - 22) sts for back neck, work rem sts, and place on a 2nd holder for other shoulder.

FRONT

Work same as back until piece measures 10 (11 - 12 - 13)″ / 25 (28 - 30 - 33) cm from beg or 2″ / 5 cm less than length of back. **Shape neck:** *Next row (RS):* K19 (20 - 21 - 22) sts, join 2nd ball of yarn and bind off center 9 (11 - 12 - 14) sts, k to end. Working both sides at same time, bind off from each neck edge 2 sts once, then 1 st twice—15 (16 - 17 - 18) sts rem each side. Work even until piece measures same length as back. Place rem on holders.

SHOULDER SEAMS

For each shoulder, k seam tog as foll: Sl front and back shoulder sts from holders to 2 dpns. Hold pieces together with the wrong sides facing each other and sweater front facing you. With a 3rd dpn, k first st from front needle tog with first st from back needle, *k next st from front and back needles tog, sl first st over 2nd

st to bind off; rep from * until all sts are bound off. Cut yarn and pull end through loop.

SLEEVES

Mark for sleeves 6 (6½ - 7 - 7½)" / 15 (16.5 - 17.5 - 19) cm down from shoulder seam on front and back. With RS facing, pick up and k44 (48 - 50 - 54) sts between markers. Work in garter st for 5 rows, then dec 1 st each end on next row, then every 6th row 2 (7 - 10 - 13) times more, then every 4th row 8 (4 - 2 - 0) times—22 (24 - 24 - 26) sts rem. Work even until sleeve measures 9 (11 - 12½ - 14)" / 23 (28 - 31.5 - 35.5) cm or desired length. Bind off loosely and evenly.

FINISHING

Neckband: With RS facing and circular needle, pick up and k46 (50 - 52 - 56) sts evenly around neck edge. Join and work in garter st (p1 rnd, k1 rnd) for 1" / 2.5 cm. Bind off loosely. Sew side and sleeve seams.

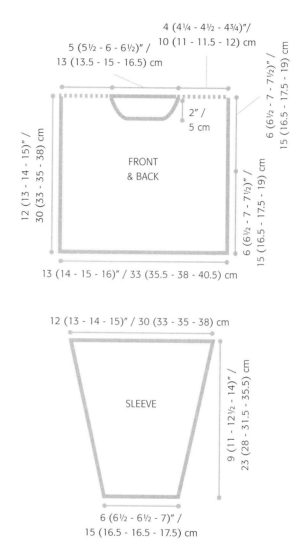

Garter-T | Adult

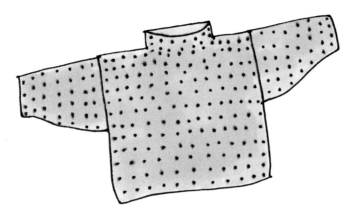

BACK

With straight needles, cast on 72 (79 - 86) sts. Work garter st (k every row) for 18 (18½ - 19)" / 45.5 (47 - 48) cm or desired length to shoulder. Work 22 (25 - 28) sts and place on a holder for one shoulder, bind off next 28 (29 - 30) sts for back neck, work rem sts, and place on a 2nd holder for other shoulder.

FRONT

Work as for back until piece measures 15½ (16 - 16½)" / 39 (40.5 - 41.5) cm from beg or 2½" / 6 cm less than length of back. **Shape**

neck: *Next row (RS):* Work 29 (32 - 35) sts, join 2nd ball of yarn and bind off center 14 (15 - 16) sts, work to end. Working both sides at same time, bind off from each neck edge 3 sts once, 2 sts once, then 1 st twice—22 (25 - 28) sts rem each side. Work even until piece measures same length as back. Place rem on holders.

SHOULDER SEAMS

For each shoulder, k seam tog as foll: Sl front and back shoulder sts from holders to 2 dpns. Hold pieces together with the wrong sides facing each other and sweater front facing you. With a 3rd dpn, k first st from front needle tog with first st from back needle, *k next st from front and back needles tog, sl first st over 2nd st to bind off; rep from * until all sts are bound off. Cut yarn and pull end through loop.

SLEEVES

Mark for sleeves 8½ (9 - 9½)" / 21.5 (23 - 24) cm down from shoulder seam on front and back. With RS facing, pick up and k62 (66 - 68) sts between markers. Work in garter st for 5 rows, then dec 1 st each end on next row, then every 8th row 12 (6 - 3) times more, then every 6th row 1 (9 - 13) times—34 sts rem. Work even until sleeve measures 18" / 45.5 cm or desired length. Bind off loosely and evenly.

FINISHING

Neckband: With RS facing and circular needle, pick up and k70 (72 - 74) sts evenly around neck edge. Join and work in garter st (p1 rnd, k1 rnd) for 3" / 7.5 cm. Bind off loosely. Sew side and sleeve seams.

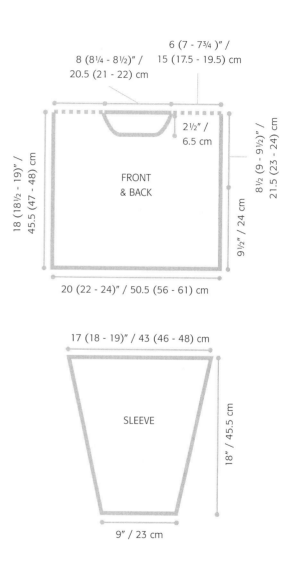

6 (7 - 7¾)" / 15 (17.5 - 19.5) cm

8 (8¼ - 8½)" / 20.5 (21 - 22) cm

2½" / 6.5 cm

8½ (9 - 9½)" / 21.5 (23 - 24) cm

18 (18½ - 19)" / 45.5 (47 - 48) cm

FRONT & BACK

9½" / 24 cm

20 (22 - 24)" / 50.5 (56 - 61) cm

17 (18 - 19)" / 43 (46 - 48) cm

SLEEVE

18" / 45.5 cm

9" / 23 cm

Go International

Chic and charming, clothes for the streets of
Gstaad or the mountains of Vail . . .

*Furz is adorable and a
very quick knit!
This jacket is a
warm but light
treat for big
and little girls.
Select a chunky
yarn that will not
curl in stockinette
stitch; Furz double
stranded is perfect.*

Bulky Faux Fur Jacket ▪ Women's/Girl's ▪ QuickKnit

SIZES

Child: 2 (4 - 6 - 8) years
Finished chest (buttoned): 28 (30 - 32 - 34)" /
                   71 (76 - 81 - 86) cm
Length, shoulder to hem: 14 (15 - 16 - 17)" /
                   36 (38 - 40.5 - 43) cm

Adult: small (medium - large)
Finished chest (buttoned): 42 (46 - 50)" /
                   106 (116 - 126.5) cm
Length, shoulder to hem: 22 (22½ - 23)" /
                   55.5 (57 - 58) cm

MATERIALS

Bulky weight yarn that will obtain gauge given below
Child: 310 (360 - 435 - 500) yd. / 280 (325 - 395 - 450) m
Adult: 700 (800 - 900) yd. / 630 (720 - 810) m
Note: Furz is used double stranded throughout: 6 (7 - 8 - 10) balls for child;
    14 (16 - 18) balls for adult
Knitting needles, one pair size 13 US (00 UK, 9 mm) or size needed to obtain
    gauge
Double pointed needles (dpns) size 13 US (00 UK, 9 mm)
Stitch holders and markers
4 buttons for child; 5 buttons for adult
Samples in photographs knit in Berroco Furz in #3801 Vanilla

GAUGE

11 sts and 14 rows = 4" / 10 cm in St st
If using Furz, use 2 strands of yarn held together.
Always check gauge to save time and ensure correct yardage and correct fit!

Furz | Child

BACK

Cast on 39 (42 - 45 - 48) sts. Work in St st for 14 (15 - 16 - 17)" / 36 (38 - 40.5 - 43) cm or desired length to shoulder. Work 13 (14 - 15 - 16) sts and place on a holder for right shoulder, work center 13 (14 - 15 - 16) sts and place on a separate holder for neck, work rem sts, and place on a separate holder for left shoulder.

LEFT FRONT

Cast on 23 (24 - 25 - 27) sts. Work in St st for 12 (13 - 14 - 15)" / 30.5 (33 - 35.5 - 38) cm or 2" / 5 cm less than length of back, end with a RS row. **Shape neck:** *Next row (WS):* Bind off 6 (6 - 6 - 7) sts, p to end. Cont to bind off beg of WS rows 2 sts twice—13 (14 - 15 - 16) sts rem. Work even until piece measures same as back. Place rem sts on a holder for shoulder. Place markers on front edge for 4 buttons, first

one at 1" / 2.5 cm from lower edge, last one ¾" / 2 cm below neck, and 2 others spaced evenly between.

RIGHT FRONT

Work same as left front to neck, end WS row, and *at the same time* work buttonholes opposite markers on RS rows as foll: K2, yo, k2tog. **Shape neck:** *Next row (RS):* Bind off 6 (6 - 6 - 7) sts, k to end. Cont to work neck shaping beg of RS rows as for left front. Work even until same length as back. Sl rem sts to holder.

SHOULDER SEAMS

For each shoulder, k seam tog as foll: Sl front and back shoulder sts from holders to 2 dpns. Hold pieces together with the wrong sides facing each other and sweater front facing you. With a 3rd dpn, k first st from front needle tog with first st from back needle, *k next st from front and back needles tog, sl first st over 2nd st to bind off; rep from * until all sts are bound off. Cut yarn and pull end through loop.

SLEEVES

Mark for sleeves 6 (6½ - 7 - 7½)" / 15.5 (16.5 - 17.5 - 19) cm down from shoulder seam on front and back. With RS facing, pick up and k34 (36 - 38 - 42) sts between markers. Starting with a p row, work 3 rows in St st.

Cont in St st, dec 1 st each edge on next row, then every 6th row 0 (2 - 3 - 4) times more, every 4th row 6 (4 - 4 - 4) times—20 (22 - 22 - 24) sts rem. Work even until sleeve measures 9 (10½ - 12 - 13½)" / 23 (26.5 - 30.5 - 34) cm or desired length. Bind off loosely and evenly knitwise.

FINISHING

Sew side and sleeve seams. **Neck edging:** With RS facing, pick up and k11 sts along right neck edge, k13 (14 - 15 - 16) sts from back holder, pick up and k11 sts along left neck edge—35 (36 - 37 - 38) sts rem. Work 3 rows rev St st. Bind off loosely and evenly. Sew on buttons.

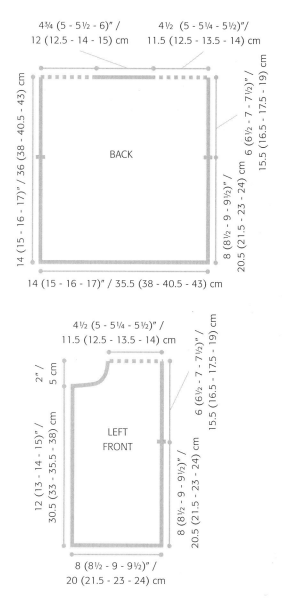

4¾ (5 - 5½ - 6)" / 12 (12.5 - 14 - 15) cm

4½ (5 - 5¼ - 5½)" / 11.5 (12.5 - 13.5 - 14) cm

6 (6½ - 7 - 7½)" / 15.5 (16.5 - 17.5 - 19) cm

14 (15 - 16 - 17)" / 36 (38 - 40.5 - 43) cm

BACK

8 (8½ - 9 - 9½)" / 20.5 (21.5 - 23 - 24) cm

14 (15 - 16 - 17)" / 35.5 (38 - 40.5 - 43) cm

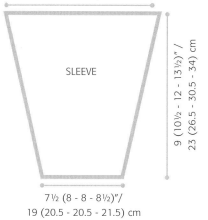

12 (13 - 14 - 15)" / 31 (33 - 35 - 38) cm

SLEEVE

9 (10½ - 12 - 13½)" / 23 (26.5 - 30.5 - 34) cm

7½ (8 - 8 - 8½)" / 19 (20.5 - 20.5 - 21.5) cm

4½ (5 - 5¼ - 5½)" / 11.5 (12.5 - 13.5 - 14) cm

2" / 5 cm

6 (6½ - 7 - 7½)" / 15.5 (16.5 - 17.5 - 19) cm

LEFT FRONT

12 (13 - 14 - 15)" / 30.5 (33 - 35.5 - 38) cm

8 (8½ - 9 - 9½)" / 20.5 (21.5 - 23 - 24) cm

8 (8½ - 9 - 9½)" / 20 (21.5 - 23 - 24) cm

Furz | Adult

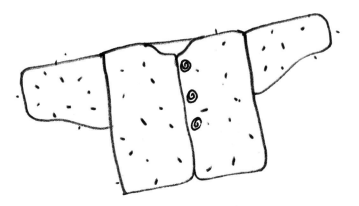

Seed St

Row 1 (RS): *K1, p1; rep from * to end.
Row 2: K the p sts and p the k sts.
Rep row 2 for seed st.

BACK

Cast on 59 (64 - 70) sts. Work in seed st for 2″ / 5 cm. Cont in St st until piece measures 22 (22½ - 23)″ / 55.5 (57 - 58) cm or desired length to shoulder. Work 20 (22 - 25) sts and place on a holder for right shoulder, work center 19 (20 - 20) sts and place on a separate holder for neck, work rem sts, and place on a separate holder for left shoulder.

LEFT FRONT

Cast on 33 (35 - 38) sts. Work in seed st for 2″ / 5 cm. Cont in St st until piece measures 19½ (20 - 20½)″ / 49 (50.5 - 51.5) cm, or 2½″ / 6 cm less than length of back; end with

a RS row. **Shape neck:** *Next row (WS):* Bind off 5 sts, p to end. Cont to bind off beg of WS rows 3 sts twice, 2 sts once—20 (22 - 25) sts rem. Work even until piece measures same as back. Place rem sts on a holder for shoulder. Place markers on front edge for 5 buttons, first one at 1″ / 2.5 cm from lower edge, last one ¾″ / 2 cm below neck, and 3 others spaced evenly between.

RIGHT FRONT

Work same as left front to neck, end WS row, and *at the same time* work buttonholes opposite markers on RS rows as foll: K2, yo, k2tog. **Shape neck:** *Next row (RS):* Bind off 5 sts, k to end. Cont to work neck shaping beg of RS rows as for left front. Work even until same length as back. Sl rem sts to holder.

SHOULDER SEAMS

For each shoulder, k seam tog as foll: Sl front and back shoulder sts from holders to 2 dpns. Hold pieces together with the wrong sides facing each other and sweater front facing you. With a 3rd dpn, k first st from front needle tog with first st from back needle, *k next st from front and back needles tog, sl first st over 2nd st to bind off; rep from * until all sts are bound off. Cut yarn and pull end through loop.

SLEEVES

Mark for sleeves 9½ (10 - 10½)″ / 24 (25.5 - 26.5) cm down from shoulder seam on front and back. With RS facing, pick up and k54 (56 - 60) sts between markers. Starting with a p row, work 3 rows in St st. Cont in St st, dec 1 st each edge on next row, then every 6th row 4 (2 - 0) times more, every 4th row 8 (11 - 14) times—28 (28 - 30) sts rem. Work even until sleeve measures 18½" / 47 cm or desired length. Bind off loosely and evenly knitwise.

FINISHING

Sew side and sleeve seams. **Neck edging:** With RS facing, pick up and k17 sts along right neck edge, k19 (20 - 20) sts from back holder, pick up and k17 sts along left neck edge—53 (54 - 54) sts. Work 3 rows rev St st. Bind off loosely and evenly. Sew on buttons.

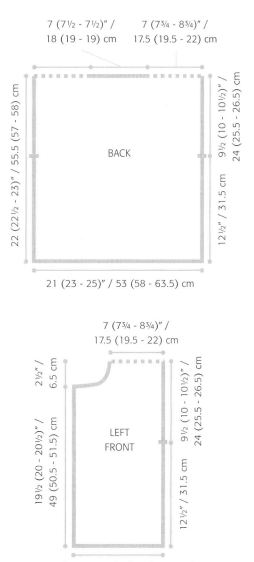

7 (7½ - 7½)" / 18 (19 - 19) cm

7 (7¾ - 8¾)" / 17.5 (19.5 - 22) cm

BACK

22 (22½ - 23)" / 55.5 (57 - 58) cm

9½ (10 - 10½)" / 24 (25.5 - 26.5) cm

12½" / 31.5 cm

21 (23 - 25)" / 53 (58 - 63.5) cm

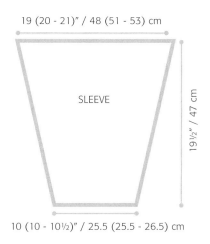

19 (20 - 21)" / 48 (51 - 53) cm

SLEEVE

19½" / 47 cm

10 (10 - 10½)" / 25.5 (25.5 - 26.5) cm

7 (7¾ - 8¾)" / 17.5 (19.5 - 22) cm

2½" / 6.5 cm

LEFT FRONT

19½ (20 - 20½)" / 49 (50.5 - 51.5) cm

9½ (10 - 10½)" / 24 (25.5 - 26.5) cm

12½" / 31.5 cm

11½ (12½ - 13½)" / 29 (31.5 - 34) cm

Nordica

This jacket is perfect for the sportsters in your life, with buttons for the little ones, a zipper for the big. I often hear knitters say they are wary of zippers; simply sew it in by hand, for easy and perfect results—really!

Wool Garter Stitch Jacket ▪ Unisex ▪ QuickKnit

SIZES

Child: 2 (4 - 6 - 8) years
Finished chest: 25 (28 - 31 - 34)″ / 63 (71 - 79 - 86.5) cm
Length, shoulder to hem: 14 (16 - 17 - 18)″ /
                        35.5 (40.5 - 43 - 46) cm

Adult: small (medium - large)
Finished chest: 42 (46 - 50)″ / 106 (116.5 - 127) cm
Length, shoulder to hem: 25½ (26 - 26½)″ /
                        64.5 (66 - 67) cm

MATERIALS

Aran weight wool that will obtain gauge given below
Child: 380 (435 - 575 - 665) yd. / 345 (395 - 520 - 490) m
    (MC)
90 (95 - 100 - 105) yd. / 80 (85 - 90 - 95) m (CC)
Adult: 1360 (1450 - 1585) yd. / 1255 (1305 - 1430) m (MC)
200 (210 - 230) yd. / 180 (190 - 210) m (CC)
Knitting needles, size 10 US (4 UK, 6 mm) or size needed to
    obtain gauge
Double pointed needles (dpns) size 10 US (4 UK, 6 mm)
Five ⅞″ / 2 cm buttons for child; 24″ / 60 cm zipper for adult
Samples in photographs knit in Manos del Uruguay in #51
    Jade (MC) and #08 Black (CC) for child; #13 Hunter
    (MC) and #08 Black (CC) for adult

GAUGE

16 sts and 32 rows = 4″ / 10 cm in garter st
Always check gauge to save time and ensure correct yardage and correct fit!

Nordica | Child

BACK

With MC, cast on 50 (56 - 62 - 68) sts. Work in garter st (k every row) for 13½ (15½ - 16½ - 17½)" / 34 (39 - 41.5 - 44.5) cm or desired length to shoulder. *Next row:* Work 15 (17 - 20 - 22) sts for one shoulder and place on a holder, bind off next 20 (22 - 22 - 24) sts for neck, work rem sts, and place on a holder for 2nd shoulder.

LEFT FRONT

With MC, cast on 24 (27 - 30 - 33) sts. Work in garter st for 11½ (13½ - 14½ - 15½)" / 30 (35 - 37.5 - 40) cm or 2" / 5 cm less than length of back, end with RS row. **Shape neck:** *Next row (WS):* Bind off 4 (4 - 4 - 5) sts, k to end. Cont to bind off beg of WS rows 2 sts twice, then 1 st 1 (2 - 2 - 2) time—15 (17 - 20 - 22) sts rem. Work even until same length as back. Place rem sts on a holder for shoulder.

RIGHT FRONT

Work as for left front to neck; end WS row. **Shape neck:** *Next row (RS):* Bind off 4 (4 - 4 - 5) sts at beg of next row. Cont to work neck shaping beg of RS rows as for left front. Work even until same length as back. Place rem sts on a holder.

SHOULDER SEAMS

For each shoulder, k seam tog as foll: Sl front and back shoulder sts from holders to 2 dpns. Hold pieces together with wrong sides facing each other and sweater front facing you. With a 3rd dpn, k first st from front needle tog with first st from back needle, *k next st from front and back needles tog, sl first st over 2nd st to bind off; rep from * until all sts are bound off. Cut yarn and pull end through loop.

SLEEVES

Place markers 6½ (7 - 7½ - 8)" / 16.5 (17.5 - 19 - 20.5) cm down from shoulder seams on front and back for armholes. With RS facing and MC, pick up and k52 (56 - 60 - 64) sts between markers. Work in garter st as foll: Work 5 rows even, then dec 1 st each side on next row, then every 6th row 11 (12 - 14 - 15) times more—28 (30 - 30 - 32) sts rem. Work even until sleeve measures 9½ (10½ - 12 - 13)" / 24 (26.5 - 30.5 - 33) cm. Join CC and k 3 rows. Bind off all sts loosely and evenly with CC.

FINISHING

Sew side and sleeve seams. **Lower edging:** With RS facing and CC, pick up and k1 st in each cast-on st along lower edge of left front, back, and right front. K 3 rows. Bind off knitwise. **Neckband:** With RS facing and CC, pick up and k46 (50 - 50 - 54) sts evenly around neck edge and work as for lower edging. **Button band** (work along left front for girl's, right front for boy's): With RS facing and CC, pick up and k46 (52 - 56 - 60) sts evenly along front edge. K 4 rows. Bind off loosely. Place markers on band for 5 buttons, first one ½" / 1.5 cm from bottom edge, last one at ½" / 1.5 cm from neck edge, and 3 others spaced evenly between. **Buttonhole band:** Work same as button band along opposite edge, working buttonholes on 2nd row opposite markers as foll: Bind off 2 sts for each buttonhole. *Next row:* Cast on 2 sts over bound-off sts. K 1 row. Bind off. Sew on buttons.

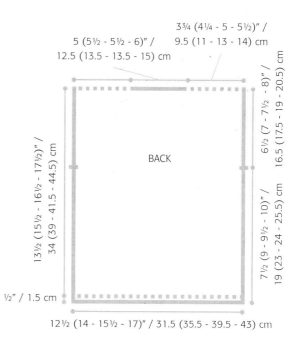

3¾ (4¼ - 5 - 5½)" /
9.5 (11 - 13 - 14) cm

5 (5½ - 5½ - 6)" /
12.5 (13.5 - 13.5 - 15) cm

BACK

13½ (15½ - 16½ - 17½)" /
34 (39 - 41.5 - 44.5) cm

6½ (7 - 7½ - 8)" /
16.5 (17.5 - 19 - 20.5) cm

7½ (9 - 9½ - 10)" /
19 (23 - 24 - 25.5) cm

½" / 1.5 cm

12½ (14 - 15½ - 17)" / 31.5 (35.5 - 39.5 - 43) cm

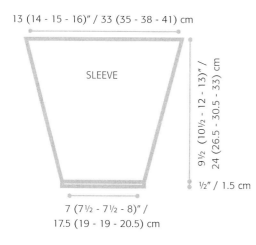

13 (14 - 15 - 16)" / 33 (35 - 38 - 41) cm

SLEEVE

9½ (10½ - 12 - 13)" /
24 (26.5 - 30.5 - 33) cm

½" / 1.5 cm

7 (7½ - 7½ - 8)" /
17.5 (19 - 19 - 20.5) cm

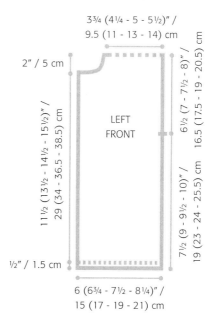

3¾ (4¼ - 5 - 5½)" /
9.5 (11 - 13 - 14) cm

2" / 5 cm

LEFT
FRONT

11½ (13½ - 14½ - 15½)" /
29 (34 - 36.5 - 38.5) cm

6½ (7 - 7½ - 8)" /
16.5 (17.5 - 19 - 20.5) cm

7½ (9 - 9½ - 10)" /
19 (23 - 24 - 25.5) cm

½" / 1.5 cm

6 (6¾ - 7½ - 8¼)" /
15 (17 - 19 - 21) cm

Nordica | Adult

BACK

With MC, cast on 84 (92 - 100) sts. Work in garter st (k every row) for 25 (25½ - 26)″ / 63 (64.5 - 65.5) cm or desired length to shoulder. *Next row:* Work 27 (30 - 34) sts for one shoulder and place on a holder, bind off next 30 (32 - 32) sts for neck, work rem sts, and place on a holder for 2nd shoulder.

LEFT FRONT

With MC, cast on 42 (46 - 50) sts. Work in garter st for 23 (23½ - 24)″ / 58 (59.5 - 60.5) cm or 2″ / 5 cm less than length of back, end with RS row. **Shape neck:** *Next row (WS):* Bind off 4 (5 - 5) sts, p to end. Cont to bind off beg of WS rows 3 sts twice, 2 sts twice, 1 st once— 27 (30 - 34) sts rem. Work even until same length as back. Place rem sts on a holder for shoulder.

RIGHT FRONT

Work as for left front to neck, end WS row. **Shape neck:** *Next row (RS):* Bind off 4 (5 - 5) sts at beg of next row. Cont to work neck shaping beg of RS rows as for left front. Work even until same length as back. Place rem sts on a holder.

SHOULDER SEAMS

For each shoulder, k seam tog as foll: Sl front and back shoulder sts from holders to 2 dpns. Hold pieces together with wrong sides facing each other and sweater front facing you. With a 3rd dpn, k first st from front needle tog with first st from back needle, *k next st from front and back needles tog, sl first st over 2nd st to bind off; rep from * until all sts are bound off. Cut yarn and pull end through loop.

SLEEVES

Place markers 9½ (10 - 10½)″ / 24 (25.5 - 26.5) cm down from shoulder seams on front and back for armholes. With RS facing and MC, pick up and k76 (80 - 84) sts between markers. Work in garter st as foll: Work 7 rows even, then dec 1 st each side on next row, then every 8th row 11 (17 - 17) times more, every 10th (10th - 6th) row 6 (2 - 4) times—40 sts rem. Work even until sleeve measures 20½ (21½ - 22)″ / 52 (54.5 - 56) cm or desired

length. Join CC and k 3 rows. Bind off all sts
loosely with CC.

FINISHING

Sew sleeve and side seams. **Lower edging:** With
RS facing and CC, pick up and k1 st in each
cast-on st along lower edge of left front, back
and right front. K 3 rows. Bind off knitwise.
Neckband: With RS facing and CC, pick up
and k sts evenly around neck edge and work as
for lower edging. **Front bands:** With RS facing
and CC, pick up and k1 st in every garter
ridge, including side edge of lower edge and
neckband. K 3 rows. Bind off. Sew in zipper.

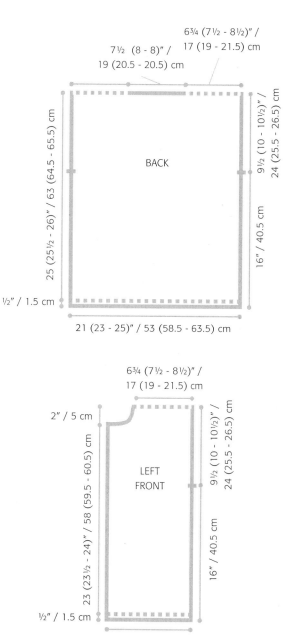

6¾ (7½ - 8½)" /
17 (19 - 21.5) cm

7½ (8 - 8)" /
19 (20.5 - 20.5) cm

BACK

9½ (10 - 10½)" /
24 (25.5 - 26.5) cm

25 (25½ - 26)" / 63 (64.5 - 65.5) cm

16" / 40.5 cm

½" / 1.5 cm

21 (23 - 25)" / 53 (58.5 - 63.5) cm

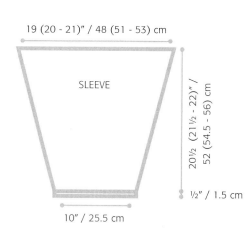

19 (20 - 21)" / 48 (51 - 53) cm

SLEEVE

20½ (21½ - 22)" /
52 (54.5 - 56) cm

½" / 1.5 cm

10" / 25.5 cm

6¾ (7½ - 8½)" /
17 (19 - 21.5) cm

2" / 5 cm

LEFT
FRONT

9½ (10 - 10½)" /
24 (25.5 - 26.5) cm

23 (23½ - 24)" / 58 (59.5 - 60.5) cm

16" / 40.5 cm

½" / 1.5 cm

10½ (11½ - 12½)" / 26.5 (29 - 31.5) cm

Chin Chin

The garter stitch gives this cotton sweater a perfect all-over weight, without edge finishing. Everyone loved this sweater; the models wanted to buy it! It is simple to knit, even the tiny left front. Yarn and buttons make a difference here, so choose carefully.

SIZES

Child: 2 (4 - 6 - 8) years
Finished chest (buttoned): 26 (29 - 32 - 35)" /
                    66 (74 - 82 - 88.5) cm
Length, shoulder to hem: 14 (15 - 16 - 17)" /
                    36 (38 - 40.5 - 43) cm

Adult: small (medium - large)
Finished bust (buttoned): 40 (44 - 48)" /
                    101 (112 - 122) cm
Length, shoulder to hem: 22 (23 - 24)" /
                    56 (58 - 61) cm

MATERIALS

Worsted weight yarn that will obtain gauge given below
Child: 680 (775 - 970 - 1150) yd. / 610 (700 - 875 - 1035) m
Adult: 1380 (1550 - 1730) yd. / 1240 (1395 - 1560) m
Knitting needles, one pair size 5 US (9 UK, 3.75 mm) or size
    needed to obtain gauge
Double pointed needles (dpns) size 5 US (9 UK, 3.75 mm)
Stitch holders
8 (8 - 9 - 9) buttons for child; 5 buttons for adult
Samples in photographs knit in Berroco Sprite #7815 Yellow
    and #7817 Red

GAUGE

20 sts and 40 rows = 4" or 10 cm in garter st
Always check gauge to save time and ensure correct yardage and correct fit!

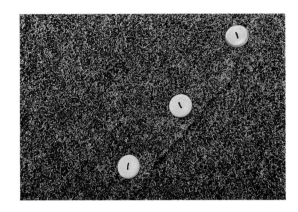

Chin Chin | Child

BACK

Cast on 65 (73 - 80 - 88) sts. Work in garter st for 14 (15 - 16 - 17)″ / 36 (38 - 40.5 - 43) cm. Work 21 (24 - 26 - 29) sts and place on a holder for right shoulder, bind off next 23 (25 - 28 - 30) sts for neck, work rem sts, and place on a separate holder for left shoulder.

LEFT FRONT

Cast on 38 (41 - 45 - 49) sts. Work in garter st for 12 (13 - 14 - 15)″ / 31 (33 - 35.5 - 38) cm; end with a RS row. **Shape neck:** *Next row (WS):* Bind off 9 (9 - 10 - 10) sts, k to end. Cont to bind off beg of WS rows 3 sts once, 2 sts 1 (1 - 1 - 2) time, dec 1 st every other row 3 (3 - 4 - 3) times—21 (24 - 26 - 29) sts rem. Work even until same length as back. Place rem sts on holder.

RIGHT FRONT

Note: Buttonhole rows: On RS rows, work k2, yo, k2tog, k rem sts. On WS rows, k to last 4 sts, k2tog, yo, k2.

Cast on 65 (73 - 80 - 88) sts. Work in garter st for 2 rows. *Next row (RS):* Work buttonhole row. Cont to work buttonhole row every 18th (20th - 19th - 21st) row 6 (6 - 7 - 7) times more, and *at the same time*, when piece measures 6 (6½ - 7 - 7½)″ / 15.5 (16.5 - 17.5 - 19) cm, from beg, end with a WS row and work as foll: **Shape sloped edge:** *Next row (RS):* K5, k2tog, k to end. Cont to dec 1 st at sloped edge every 4th row 6 (6 - 4 - 2) times more, every other row 17 (20 - 26 - 33) times—41 (46 - 49 - 52) sts rem. Work even until piece measures 12 (13 - 14 - 15)″ / 31 (33 - 35.5 - 38) cm from beg; end with a WS row. **Shape neck:** *Next row (RS):* Bind off 11 (11 - 12 - 12) sts, (neck edge), k to end. Cont to bind off from neck edge 3 sts once, 2 sts 1 (2- 2- 2) times, dec 1 st every other row 4 times—21 (24 - 26 - 29) sts rem. Work even until front measures same length as back. Place rem sts on holder.

SHOULDER SEAMS

For each shoulder, k seam tog as foll: Sl front and back shoulder sts from holders to 2 dpns. Hold pieces together with wrong sides facing each other and sweater front facing you. With a 3rd dpn, k first st from front needle tog with first st from back needle, *k next st from front and back needles tog, sl first st over 2nd st to bind off; rep from * until all sts are bound off. Cut yarn and pull end through loop.

SLEEVES

Mark for sleeves 6 (6½ - 7 - 7½)″ / 15.5 (16.5 - 17.5 - 19) cm down from shoulder

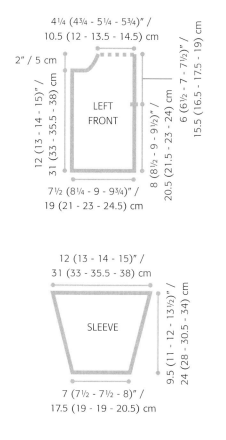

4¼ (4¾ - 5¼ - 5¾)" /
10.5 (12 - 13.5 - 14.5) cm

2" / 5 cm

LEFT
FRONT

12 (13 - 14 - 15)" /
31 (33 - 35.5 - 38) cm

8 (8½ - 9 - 9½)" /
20.5 (21.5 - 23 - 24) cm

6 (6½ - 7 - 7½)" /
15.5 (16.5 - 17.5 - 19) cm

7½ (8¼ - 9 - 9¾)" /
19 (21 - 23 - 24.5) cm

12 (13 - 14 - 15)" /
31 (33 - 35.5 - 38) cm

SLEEVE

9.5 (11 - 12 - 13½)" /
24 (28 - 30.5 - 34) cm

7 (7½ - 7½ - 8)" /
17.5 (19 - 19 - 20.5) cm

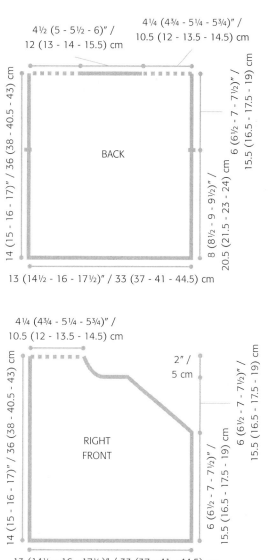

4½ (5 - 5½ - 6)" /
12 (13 - 14 - 15.5) cm

4¼ (4¾ - 5¼ - 5¾)" /
10.5 (12 - 13.5 - 14.5) cm

BACK

14 (15 - 16 - 17)" / 36 (38 - 40.5 - 43) cm

8 (8½ - 9 - 9½)" /
20.5 (21.5 - 23 - 24) cm

6 (6½ - 7 - 7½)" /
15.5 (16.5 - 17.5 - 19) cm

13 (14½ - 16 - 17½)" / 33 (37 - 41 - 44.5) cm

4¼ (4¾ - 5¼ - 5¾)" /
10.5 (12 - 13.5 - 14.5) cm

2" /
5 cm

RIGHT
FRONT

14 (15 - 16 - 17)" / 36 (38 - 40.5 - 43) cm

6 (6½ - 7 - 7½)" /
15.5 (16.5 - 17.5 - 19) cm

6 (6½ - 7 - 7½)" /
15.5 (16.5 - 17.5 - 19) cm

13 (14½ - 16 - 17½)" / 33 (37 - 41 - 44.5) cm

seam on front and back. With RS facing, pick up and k60 (66 - 70 - 76) sts between markers. Working in garter st, work 7 rows even. Dec 1 st each edge on next row, then every 8th row 6 (7 - 6 - 8) times more, every 6th row 5 (6 - 9 - 9) times—36 (38 - 38 - 40) sts rem. Work even until sleeve measures 9½ (11 - 12 - 13½)" / 24 (28 - 30.5 - 34) cm. Bind off loosely and evenly knitwise.

FINISHING

Neckband: With RS facing, beg at right front neck edge, pick up and k72 (76 - 82 - 86) sts evenly around neck edge. Work in garter st for 5 rows. *Next row:* K2, yo, k2tog, k rem sts.

Work even until band measures 1" / 2.5 cm. Bind off. Sew side and sleeve seams. Sew on buttons.

Chin Chin | Adult

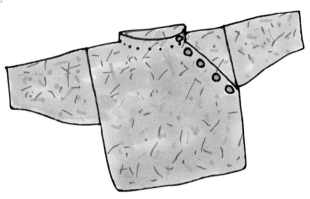

BACK

Cast on 100 (110 - 120) sts. Work in garter st (k all rows) for 22 (23 - 24)" / 56 (58 - 61) cm. K31 (36 - 40) sts and place on a holder for right shoulder, bind off next 38 (38 - 40) sts for neck, k rem sts, and place on a separate holder for left shoulder.

LEFT FRONT

Cast on 9 (9 - 11) sts. Work in garter st, inc 1 st at beg of every WS row 30 (35 - 39) times—39 (44 - 50) sts rem. Work even until piece measures 8 (8½ - 9)" / 20.5 (21.5 - 23) cm from beg; end with a RS row. **Shape neck:** *Next row (WS):* Bind off 2 sts (neck edge), k to end. Cont to bind off from neck edge 2 sts 1 (1 - 2) times more, dec 1 st every other row 4 times—31 (36 - 40) sts rem. Work even until front measures 10½ (11 - 11½)" / 27 (28 - 29.5) cm from beg. Place rem sts on a holder.

RIGHT FRONT

Cast on 100 (110 - 120) sts. Work in garter st for 12½ (13 - 13½)" / 31.5 (32.5 - 34) cm; end with a WS row. **Buttonhole row (RS):** K3, bind

off 2 sts, k to end. *Next row:* Cast on 2 sts over bound-off sts. Cont to work buttonhole row every 18th (20th - 22nd) row 3 times more, and *at the same time*, when piece measures 13 (13½ - 14)" / 33 (34 - 35.5) cm from beg, end with a WS row and work as foll: **Shape sloped edge:** *All RS rows:* k2tog, k to end. *All WS rows:* K to last 7 sts, k2tog, k5. Cont to dec 1 st at sloped edge every row 19 (23 - 29) times more, every other row 22 (23 - 22) times—58 (63 - 68) sts rem. Work even until piece measures 19½ (20½ - 21½)" / 49.5 (51.5 - 54.5) cm from beg; end with a WS row. **Shape neck:** *Next row (RS):* Bind off 14 (14 - 15) sts (neck edge), k to end. Cont to bind off from neck edge 3 sts twice, 2 sts twice, dec 1 st every other row 3 times—31 (36 - 40) sts rem. Work even until front measures same length as back. Place rem sts on a holder.

SHOULDER SEAMS

For each shoulder, k seam tog as foll: Sl front and back shoulder sts from holders to 2 dpns. Hold pieces together with wrong sides facing each other and sweater front facing you. With a 3rd dpn, k first st from front needle tog with first st from back needle, *k next st from front and back needles tog, sl first st over 2nd st to bind off; rep from * until all sts are bound off. Cut yarn and pull end through loop.

SLEEVES

Mark for sleeves 9 (9½ - 10)" / 23 (24 - 25.5) cm down from shoulder seam on front and back. With RS facing, pick up and k90 (96 -

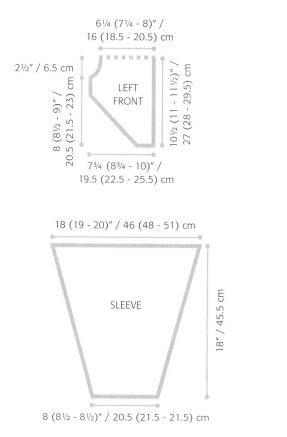

6¼ (7¼ - 8)" /
16 (18.5 - 20.5) cm

2½" / 6.5 cm

LEFT
FRONT

8 (8½ - 9)" /
20.5 (21.5 - 23) cm

10½ (11 - 11½)" /
27 (28 - 29.5) cm

7¾ (8¾ - 10)" /
19.5 (22.5 - 25.5) cm

18 (19 - 20)" / 46 (48 - 51) cm

SLEEVE

18" / 45.5 cm

8 (8½ - 8½)" / 20.5 (21.5 - 21.5) cm

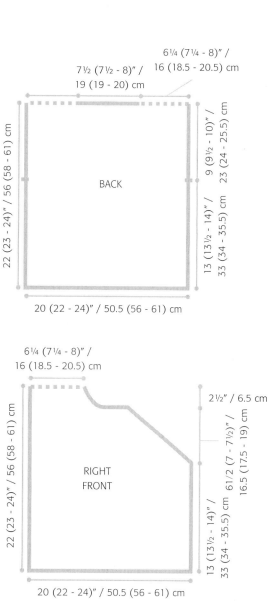

7½ (7½ - 8)" /
19 (19 - 20) cm

6¼ (7¼ - 8)" /
16 (18.5 - 20.5) cm

BACK

9 (9½ - 10)" /
23 (24 - 25.5) cm

22 (23 - 24)" / 56 (58 - 61) cm

13 (13½ - 14)" /
33 (34 - 35.5) cm

20 (22 - 24)" / 50.5 (56 - 61) cm

6¼ (7¼ - 8)" /
16 (18.5 - 20.5) cm

2½" / 6.5 cm

RIGHT
FRONT

6½ (7 - 7½)" /
16.5 (17.5 - 19) cm

22 (23 - 24)" / 56 (58 - 61) cm

13 (13½ - 14)" /
33 (34 - 35.5) cm

20 (22 - 24)" / 50.5 (56 - 61) cm

100) sts between markers. Work 7 rows garter st. Dec 1 st each edge on next row, then every 8th (8th - 4th) row 9 (3 - 3) times more, every 6th row 15 (23 - 25) times—40 (42 - 42) sts rem. Work even until sleeve measures 18" / 45.5 cm. Bind off loosely and evenly knitwise.

FINISHING

Neckband: With RS facing, beg at right front neck edge, pick up and k78 (78 - 82) sts evenly around neck edge. Work in garter st for 5 rows. *Next row (RS):* K3, bind off 2, k rem sts. *Next row:* Cast on 2 sts over bound-off sts. Work even until band measures 1" / 2.5 cm. Bind off. Sew side and sleeve seams. Sew on buttons.

Winter Argyle

This simple patterning presents a powerful all-over effect. Make sure you think "loose and easy" when you carry your yarn to avoid puckering. The fold-under hemming makes a neat and unexpected finish.

Worsted Wool Pullover with Diamond Pattern ▪ Unisex ▪ Fair Isle

SIZES

Child: 2/3 (4/6 - 8/10) years
Finished chest: 29 (33 - 37)" / 72.5 (82.5 - 92.5) cm
Length, shoulder to hem: 14 (16 - 18)" /
35 (41 - 46) cm

Adult: small (medium - large)
Finished chest: 48½ (52½ - 56½)" /
123 (133 - 143) cm
Length, shoulder to hem: 25½ (26 - 26½)" /
64.5 (66 - 67.5) cm

MATERIALS

Worsted weight wool that will obtain gauge given below
Child: 395 (515 - 650) yd. / 355 (465 - 585) m (MC)
115 (150 - 185) yd. / 105 (135 - 165) m (CC)
Adult: 1240 (1330 - 1420) yd. / 1115 (1200 - 1280) m (MC)
355 (380 - 405) yd. / 320 (340 - 365) m (CC)
Knitting needles sizes 7 and 8 US (7 and 6 UK, 4.5 and 5 mm) or size needed
 to obtain gauge
Double pointed needles (dpns) size 8 US (6 UK, 5 mm)
Circular needle size 7 US (7 UK, 4.5 mm), 16" / 40 cm
Stitch holders and markers
Samples in photographs knit in Brown Sheep #M05 Onyx (MC) and #M11
 White Frost (CC)

GAUGE

20 sts and 20 rows = 4" or 10 cm over St st and chart pat using size 8 US (6
 UK, 5 mm) needles
Always check gauge to save time and ensure correct yardage and correct fit!

Winter Argyle | Child

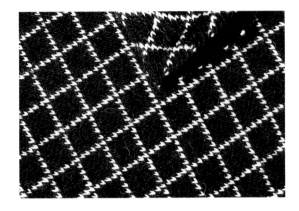

BACK

With smaller needles and MC, cast on 73 (83 - 93) sts. Work in St st for 5 rows. *Next row (WS):* K for turning ridge. Change to larger needles and work in St st and chart pat as foll: Work 1 st MC, work 10-st rep of chart 7 (8 - 9) times, work first st of rep once more, work 1 st MC. Cont in pat as est until piece measures 14 (16 - 18)″ / 35 (41 - 46) cm above turning ridge, or desired length to shoulder. With MC, work 21 (25 - 29) sts and place on a holder for one shoulder, bind off next 31 (33 - 35) sts for back neck, work rem sts, and place on a 2nd holder for other shoulder.

FRONT

Work as for back until piece measures 12 (14 - 16)″ / 30 (36 - 41) cm above turning ridge, or

2″ / 5 cm less than length of back, end WS row.
Shape neck: *Next row (RS):* Work 29 (33 - 37) sts, join 2nd ball of yarn and bind off center 15 (17 - 19) sts, work to end. Working both sides at the same time, bind off from each neck edge 3 sts once, 2 sts twice, 1 st once—21 (25 - 29) sts rem each side. Work even until same length as back, working last row with MC. Place rem sts each side on holders.

SHOULDER SEAMS

For each shoulder, k seam tog as foll: Sl front and back shoulder sts from holders to 2 dpns. Hold pieces together with wrong sides facing each other and sweater front facing you. With a 3rd dpn, k first st from front needle tog with first st from back needle, *k next st from front and back needles tog, sl first st over 2nd st to bind off; rep from * until all sts are bound off. Cut yarn and pull end through loop.

SLEEVES

Mark for sleeves 7 (8 - 9)″ / 17.5 (20.5 - 23) cm down from shoulder seam on front and back. With RS facing and larger needles, pick up and k73 (83 - 93) sts between markers. Work in St st and chart pat same as back. *At the same time,* work 3 rows even, then dec 1 st each end (working dec sts into chart pat) on

55

Winter Argyle

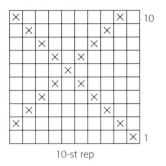

10

10-st rep

Color Key

□ MC

☒ CC

Note: Read RS
rows from right
to left, WS rows
from left to right

6 (6½ - 7)" /
15 (16.5 - 17.5) cm

4 (4¼ - 5½)" /
10.5 (12 - 14.5) cm

2" /
5 cm

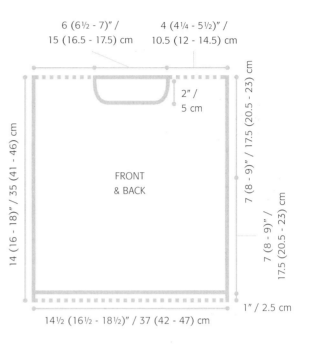

FRONT
& BACK

7 (8 - 9)" / 17.5 (20.5 - 23) cm

7 (8 - 9)" /
17.5 (20.5 - 23) cm

14 (16 - 18)" / 35 (41 - 46) cm

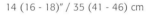

1" / 2.5 cm

14½ (16½ - 18½)" / 37 (42 - 47) cm

14 (16 - 18)" / 35 (41 - 46) cm

SLEEVE

10 (11½ - 13)" / 25.5 (29 - 33) cm

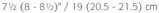

7½ (8 - 8½)" / 19 (20.5 - 21.5) cm

next row, then every 4th row 4 (4 - 5) times
more, every 2nd row 12 (16 - 18) times—39
(41 - 45) sts rem. Work even until sleeve measures 10 (11½ - 13)" / 25.5 (29 - 33) cm or
desired length; end with a RS row. Change to
smaller needles. *Next row (WS):* With MC, k
for turning ridge. Work in St st for 5 rows.
Bind off loosely and evenly.

FINISHING

Fold hem at lower edge of back, front, and
sleeves to WS and sew in place. Sew side and
sleeve seams. **Neckband:** With RS facing, circular needle, and MC, pick up and k64 (68 - 72)
sts evenly around neck edge. Join and work in
k1, p1 rib for 3 rows. Bind off in rib.

Winter Argyle | Adult

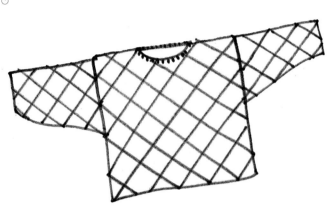

BACK

With smaller needles and MC, cast on 123 (133 - 143) sts. Work in St st for 5 rows. *Next row (WS):* K for turning ridge. Change to larger needles and work in St st and chart pat as foll: Work 1 st MC, work 10-st rep of chart 12 (13 - 14) times, work first st of rep once more, work 1 st MC. Cont in pat as est until piece measures 25½ (26 - 26½)" / 64.5 (66 - 67.5) cm above turning ridge, or desired length to shoulder. With MC, work 39 (44 - 48) sts and place on a holder for one shoulder, bind off next 45 (45 - 47) sts for back neck, work rem sts, and place on a 2nd holder for other shoulder.

FRONT

Work as for back until piece measures 22½ (23 - 23½)" / 57 (58.5 - 60) above turning ridge, or

3" / 7.5 cm less than length of back; end WS row. **Shape neck:** *Next row (RS):* Work 51 (56 - 60) sts, join 2nd ball of yarn, and bind off center 21 (21 - 23) sts; work to end. Working both sides at same time, bind off from each neck edge 3 sts twice, 2 sts twice, 1 st twice— 39 (44 - 48) sts rem each side. Work even until same length as back, working last row with MC. Place rem sts each side on holders.

SHOULDER SEAMS

For each shoulder, k seam tog as foll: Sl front and back shoulder sts from holders to 2 dpns. Hold pieces together with wrong sides facing each other and sweater front facing you. With a 3rd dpn, k first st from front needle tog with first st from back needle, *k next st from front and back needles tog, sl first st over 2nd st to bind off; rep from * until all sts are bound off. Cut yarn and pull end through loop.

SLEEVES

Mark for sleeves 12" / 30.5 cm down from shoulder seam on front and back. With RS facing and larger needles, pick up and k123 sts between markers. Work in St st and chart pat as foll: Work 1 st MC, work 10-st rep of chart 12 times, work first st of rep once more, work 1 st MC. Cont in pat as est and *at the same time*, work 3 rows even, then dec 1 st each end

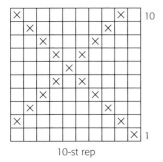

10-st rep

Color Key

☐ MC

☒ CC

Note: Read RS rows from right to left, WS rows from left to right

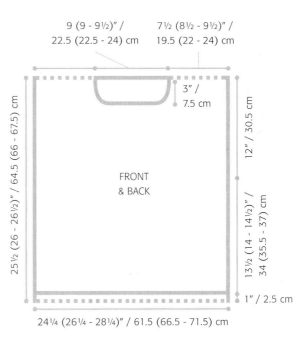

9 (9 - 9½)" / 22.5 (22.5 - 24) cm

7½ (8½ - 9½)" / 19.5 (22 - 24) cm

3" / 7.5 cm

12" / 30.5 cm

25½ (26 - 26½)" / 64.5 (66 - 67.5) cm

FRONT & BACK

13½ (14 - 14½)" / 34 (35.5 - 37) cm

1" / 2.5 cm

24¼ (26¼ - 28¼)" / 61.5 (66.5 - 71.5) cm

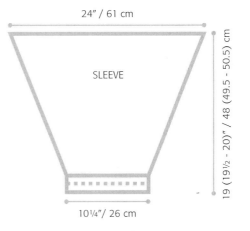

24" / 61 cm

SLEEVE

19 (19½ - 20)" / 48 (49.5 - 50.5) cm

10¼"/ 26 cm

(working dec sts into chart pat) on next row, then every 4th row 9 (10 - 11) times more, every 2nd row 25 (24 - 23) times—53 sts rem. Work even until sleeve measures 19 (19½ - 20)" / 48 (49.5 - 50.5) cm or desired length; end with a RS row. Change to smaller needles. *Next row (WS):* With MC, k for turning ridge. Work in St st for 5 rows. Bind off loosely and evenly.

FINISHING

Fold hem at lower edge of back, front, and sleeves to WS and sew in place. Sew side and sleeve seams. **Neckband:** With RS facing, circular needle, and MC, pick up and k98 (98 - 102) sts evenly around neck edge. Join and work in k1, p1 rib for 3 rows. Bind off in rib.

Celebrate

Party clothes and dress-up best for tots, teens, and even grandmothers!

Festiva

Loose and a bit boxy, this sweater has a flirty peplum to dress it up and is very easy, very chic, and perfect for holiday dressing when you want a little lift. You can make a statement with contrasting buttons.

Chenille Cardigan with Peplum ▪ Women's/Girl's ▪ QuickKnit

SIZES

Child: 2 (4 - 6 - 8) years
Finished chest (buttoned): 28 (30 - 32 - 34)" /
71 (76 - 81 - 86) cm
Length, shoulder to hem: 15 (16 - 17 - 18)" /
38 (41 - 43 - 45.5) cm

Adult: small (medium - large)
Finished chest (buttoned): 41 (44 - 47)" /
104 (111.5 - 119) cm
Length, shoulder to hem: 21 (22 - 23)" /
53.5 (55.5 - 58.5) cm

MATERIALS

Heavy weight cotton that will obtain gauge given below
Child: 415 (490 - 575 - 665) yd. / 375 (440 - 520 - 600) m
Adult: 935 (1035 - 1140) yd. / 845 (930 - 1025) m
Knitting needles size 6 US (8 UK, 4 mm) or size needed to
obtain gauge
Double pointed needles (dpns) size 6 US (8 UK, 4 mm)
Stitch holders and markers
4 buttons for child; 5 buttons for adult
*Samples in photographs knit in Crystal Palace Chenille #2230 Mango for
child; #3425 Brick for adult*

GAUGE

16 sts and 20 rows = 4" or 10 cm over St st
Always check gauge to save time and ensure correct yardage and correct fit!

Festiva | Child

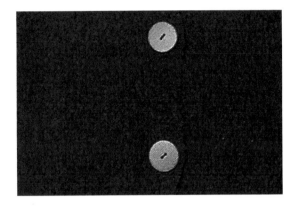

BACK

Cast on 112 (120 - 128 - 136) sts. Work in garter st (k every row) for 3 rows. Cont in St st starting with a p row until piece measures 2″ / 5 cm from beg; end with a WS row. *Peplum dec row (RS):* *K2tog; rep from * across—56 (60 - 64 - 68) sts rem. Cont in St st until piece measures 15 (16 - 17 - 18)″ / 38 (41 - 43 - 45.5) cm from beg or desired length to shoulder. Work 17 (18 - 20 - 21) sts and place on a holder for one shoulder, bind off next 22 (24 - 24 - 26) sts for back neck, work rem sts, and place on a 2nd holder for other shoulder.

LEFT FRONT

Cast on 56 (60 - 64 - 68) sts. Work in garter st for 3 rows. *Next row (WS):* K4 (garter st band), p to end. Cont in St st, keeping 4 buttonband sts in garter st until piece measures 2″ / 5 cm from beg; end with a WS row. *Next row (RS): Peplum dec row:* *K2tog; rep from * across until 4 sts rem, k4 for band—30 (32 - 34 - 36) sts rem. Cont in St st and garter st band until piece measures 13 (14 - 15 - 16)″ /

33 (36 - 38 - 40.5) cm from beg or 2″ / 5 cm less than length of back, end with a RS row. **Shape neck:** *Next row (WS):* K4 sts and place on a holder, bind off 3 (3 - 3 - 4) sts, p to end. Cont to bind off at beg of WS rows 3 sts 0 (1-1- 1) time, 2 sts 3 (2 - 2 - 2) times—17 (18 - 20 - 21) sts rem. Work even until same length as back. Place rem sts on holder. Place markers on band for 4 buttons, first one just above peplum dec row, last one ¼″ / 1 cm below neck edge, and 2 others spaced evenly between.

RIGHT FRONT

Cast on 56 (60 - 64 - 68) sts. Work in garter st for 3 rows. *Next row (WS):* P to last 4 sts, k4 for buttonhole band. Work as for left front for 2″ / 5 cm from beg; end with a WS row. *Peplum dec row: Next row (RS):* K4, *k2tog; rep from * across—30 (32 - 34 - 36) sts rem. Cont as for left front to neck, end with a WS row, and *at the same time*, work a buttonhole row opposite each marker on RS rows as foll: K2, k2tog, yo, k to end. **Shape neck:** *Next row (RS):* K4 sts and place on a holder, bind off 3 (3 - 3 - 4) sts, k to end. Cont to work neck shaping beg of RS rows as for left front. Work even until same length as back. Place rem sts on holder.

SHOULDER SEAMS

For each shoulder, k seam tog as foll: Sl front and back shoulder sts from holders to 2 dpns. Hold pieces together with wrong sides facing each other and sweater front facing you. With a 3rd dpn, k first st from front needle tog with first st from back needle, *k next st from front and back needles tog, sl first st over 2nd st to bind off; rep from * until all sts are bound off. Cut yarn and pull end through loop.

SLEEVES

Mark for sleeves 5½ (6 - 6½ - 7)" / 14 (15.5 - 16.5 - 17.5) cm down from shoulder seam on front and back. With RS facing, pick up and k44 (48 - 52 - 56) sts between markers. Starting with a p row, work 3 rows St st. Cont in St st, dec 1 st each end on next row, then every 4th row 6 (6 - 8 - 7) times more, every 6th row 2 (3 - 3 - 5) times—26 (28 - 28 - 30) sts rem. Work even until sleeve measures 9 (10½ - 12 - 13½)" / 25 (26.5 - 30.5 - 34) cm or desired length. Work in garter st for 3 rows. Bind off loosely and evenly knitwise.

FINISHING

Sew side and sleeve seams. **Neckband:** With RS facing, k4 sts from right front neck holder, pick up and k47 (51 - 51 - 55) sts evenly around neck edge, k4 from left front neck holder—55 (59 - 59 - 63) sts. Work in garter st for 3 rows. Bind off loosely and evenly knitwise.

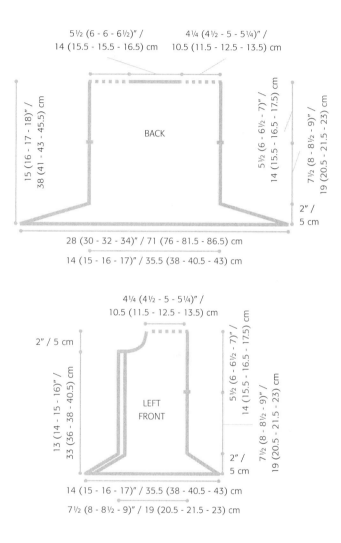

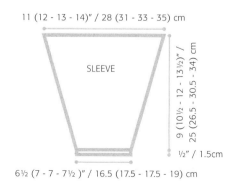

Festiva | Adult

BACK

Cast on 164 (176 - 188) sts. Work in garter st (k every row) for 3 rows. Cont in St st starting with a p row until piece measures 3″ / 7.5 cm from beg, end with a WS row. *Peplum dec row (RS):* *K2tog; rep from * across—82 (88 - 94) sts rem. Cont in St st until piece measures 21 (22 - 23)″ / 53.5 (55.5 - 58.5) cm from beg or desired length to shoulder. Work 27 (29 - 32) sts and place on a holder for one shoulder, bind off next 28 (30 - 30) sts for back neck, work rem sts, and place on a 2nd holder for other shoulder.

LEFT FRONT

Cast on 82 (88 - 94) sts. Work in garter st for 3 rows. *Next row (WS):* K4 (garter st band), p to end. Cont in St st, keeping 4 buttonband sts in garter st until piece measures 3″ / 7.5 cm from beg, end with a WS row. *Peplum dec row (RS):* *K2tog; rep from * across to last 4 sts, k4 for band—43 (46 - 49) sts rem. Cont in St st and garter st band until piece measures 18 (19 - 20)″ / 46 (48 - 51) cm from beg or 3″ / 7.5 cm

less than length of back; end with a RS row. **Shape neck:** *Next row (WS):* K4 sts and place on a holder, bind off 4 (5 - 5) sts, p to end. Cont to bind off at beg of WS rows 2 sts twice, then dec 1 st every other row 4 times—27 (29 - 32) sts rem. Work even until same length as back. Place rem sts on holder. Place markers on band for 5 buttons, first one just above peplum dec row, last one ¼″ / 1 cm below neck edge, and 3 others spaced evenly between.

RIGHT FRONT

Cast on 82 (88 - 94) sts. Work in garter st for 3 rows. *Next row (WS):* P to last 4 sts, k4 for buttonhole band. Work as for left front for 3″ / 7.5 cm from beg; end with a WS row. *Peplum dec row: Next row (RS):* K4, *k2tog; rep from * across—43 (46 - 49) sts rem. Cont as for left front to neck, end with a WS row, and *at the same time*, work a buttonhole row opposite each marker on RS rows as foll: K2, k2tog, yo, k to end. **Shape neck:** *Next row (RS):* K4 sts and place on a holder, bind off 4 (5 - 5) sts, k to end. Cont to work neck shaping beg of RS rows as for left front. Work even until same length as back. Place rem sts on holder.

SHOULDER SEAMS

For each shoulder, k seam tog as foll: Sl front and back shoulder sts from holders to 2 dpns. Hold pieces together with wrong sides facing each other and sweater front facing you. With a 3rd dpn, k first st from front needle tog with first st from back needle, *k next st from front and back needles tog, sl first st over 2nd st to bind off; rep from * until all sts are bound off. Cut yarn and pull end through loop.

SLEEVES

Mark for sleeves 9 (9½ - 10)″ / 23 (24 - 25.5) cm down from shoulder seam on front and back. With RS facing, pick up and k72 (76 - 80) sts between markers. Starting with a p row, work 3 rows St st. Cont in St st, dec 1 st each end on next row, then every 4th row 19 times more, every 2nd row 0 (1 - 2) times—32 (34 - 36) sts rem. Work even until sleeve measures 17 (17½ - 18)″ / 43 (44.5 - 45.5) cm or desired length. Work in garter st for 3 rows. Bind off loosely and evenly knitwise.

FINISHING

Sew side and sleeve seams. **Neckband:** With RS facing, k4 sts from right front neck holder, pick up and k67 (71 - 71) sts evenly around neck edge, k4 from left front neck holder—75 (79 - 79) sts. Work in garter st for 3 rows. Bind off loosely and evenly knitwise.

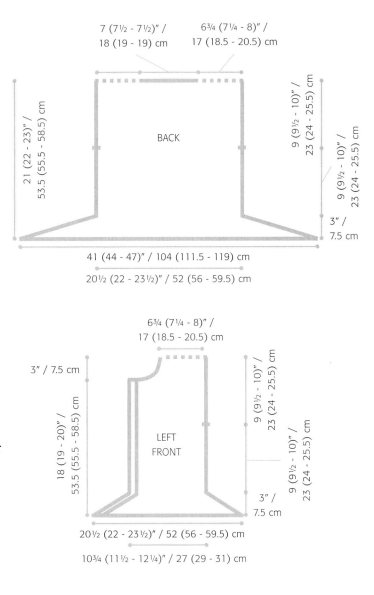

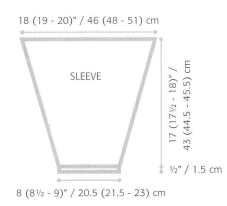

Ivy League

Quite sophisticated, this vest has been a showstopper. We knit it in Sensuwool, which gives it a lovely drape and hand. It is adorable in pint size, too, for boys or girls!

Cabled Vest ■ Unisex/Child's

SIZES

Child: 4 (6 - 8 - 10) years
Finished chest: 24 (26 - 28 - 30)" /
          61 (66 - 71 - 76) cm
Length, shoulder to hem: 15 (16½ - 18 - 19½)" /
          38 (42 - 46 - 49.5) cm

Adult: small (medium - large)
Finished chest: 42 (46 - 50)" /
          107 (117 - 127) cm
Length, shoulder to hem: 25½ (26 - 26½)" /
          64.5 (66 - 67) cm

MATERIALS

Double-knitting weight yarn that will obtain gauge given below
Child: 380 (450 - 530 - 615) yd. / 342 (405 - 477 - 555) m
Adult: 1130 (1260 - 1400) yd. / 1017 (1135 - 1260) m
Knitting needles size 7 US (7 UK, 4.5 mm) or size needed to obtain gauge
Double pointed needles (dpns) size 7 US (7 UK, 4.5 mm)
16" / 40 cm circular needle size 7 US (7 UK, 4.5 mm)
Cable needle (cn)
Stitch holders
Samples in photographs knit in Berroco Sensuwool #7645 Shaker Gray Tweed

GAUGE

24 sts and 32 rows = 4" or 10 cm over cable pat
Always check gauge to save time and ensure correct yardage and correct fit!

Ivy League | Child

Cable Pat (multiple for 14 sts plus 8)

Cable 6 = Sl next 3 sts to cn and hold in back of work, k3, k3 from cn

Row 1 (RS): *P1, k6; rep from *, end p1.

Rows 2, 4, 6, and 8: K the k sts and p the p sts.

Row 3: *P1, cable 6, p1, k6; rep from *, end p1, cable 6, p1.

Rows 5 and 7: Rep row 1.

Rep rows 1–8 for cable pat.

BACK

Cast on 71 (77 - 83 - 89) sts. Work in k1, p1 rib for 1″ / 2.5 cm, inc 1 st on last row—72 (78 - 84 - 90) sts. Work in pat as foll: *Next row (RS):* Work 4 (0 - 3 - 6) sts in St st, work cable pat on 64 (78 - 78 - 78) sts, work 4 (0 - 3 - 6) sts in St st. Cont in pats as est until piece measures 10 (11 - 12 - 13)″ / 25.5 (28 - 30.5 - 33) cm from beg or desired length to armhole. **Shape armholes:** Bind off 3 sts at beg of next 2 rows, dec 1 st each side every other row 3 times—60 (66 - 72 - 78) sts rem. Work even until armhole measures 5 (5 - 6 - 6)″ / 12.5 (14 - 15.5 - 16.5) cm; end WS row. *Next row (RS):* Work 15 (17 - 19 - 21) sts for right shoulder and place on a holder; work 30 (32 - 34 - 36) sts for back neck and place on a 2nd holder; work rem sts for left shoulder and place on a 3rd holder for later finishing.

FRONT

Work as for back to armhole; end with a WS row. **Shape armhole and neck:** *Next row (RS):* Work armhole shaping as for back, and *at the same time*, work to center, join 2nd ball of yarn, and work to end. Working both sides at same time, dec 1 st at each neck edge every other row 15 times, then every 4th row 0 (1 - 2 - 3) time—15 (17 - 19 - 21) sts rem each side. Work even until same length as back. Place rem sts on holders.

SHOULDER SEAMS

For each shoulder, k seam tog as foll: Sl front and back shoulder sts from holders to 2 dpns. Hold pieces together with the wrong sides facing each other and sweater front facing you. With a 3rd dpn, k first st from front needle tog with first st from back needle, *k next st from front and back needles tog, sl first st over 2nd st to bind off; rep from * until all sts are bound off. Cut yarn and pull end through loop.

FINISHING

Neckband: With RS facing and circular needle or dpns, k30 (32 - 34 - 36) sts from back neck holder, pick up and k38 (42 - 44 - 47) sts along left front neck, place marker, pick up 38 (42 - 44 - 47) sts along right front neck—106 (116 - 122 - 130) sts. Join and work in k1, p1 rib, dec 1 st each side of center marker every row until band measures 1″ / 2.5 cm. Bind off in rib. Sew side seams. **Armhole band:** With RS facing and dpns, pick up and k68 (76 - 82 - 90) sts evenly around each armhole edge. Join and work in k1, p1 rib for 1″ / 2.5 cm. Bind off in rib.

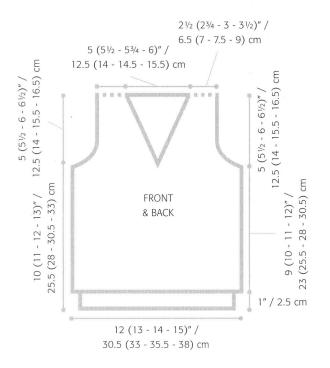

2½ (2¾ - 3 - 3½)″ /
6.5 (7 - 7.5 - 9) cm

5 (5½ - 5¾ - 6)″ /
12.5 (14 - 14.5 - 15.5) cm

5 (5½ - 6 - 6½)″ /
12.5 (14 - 15.5 - 16.5) cm

5 (5½ - 6 - 6½)″ /
12.5 (14 - 15.5 - 16.5) cm

10 (11 - 12 - 13)″ /
25.5 (28 - 30.5 - 33) cm

9 (10 - 11 - 12)″ /
23 (25.5 - 28 - 30.5) cm

FRONT & BACK

1″ / 2.5 cm

12 (13 - 14 - 15)″ /
30.5 (33 - 35.5 - 38) cm

Ivy League | Adult

Cable Pat (multiple for 14 sts plus 8)

Cable 6 = Sl next 3 sts to cn and hold in
 back of work, k3, k3 from cn

Row 1 (RS): *P1, k6; rep from *, end p1.

Rows 2, 4, 6, and 8: K the k sts and p the
 p sts.

Row 3: *P1, cable 6, p1, k6; rep from *, end
 p1, cable 6, p1.

Rows 5 and 7: Rep row 1.

Rep rows 1–8 for cable pat.

BACK

Cast on 125 (137 - 149) sts. Work in k1, p1
rib for 2″ / 5 cm, inc 1 st on last row to 126
(138 - 150) sts. Work in pat as foll: *Next row
(RS):* Work 3 (2 - 1) sts in St st, work cable pat
on 120 (134 - 148) sts, work 3 (2 - 1) sts in St
st. Cont in pats as est until piece measures 17″ /

43 cm from beg or desired length to armhole.
Shape armholes: Bind off 5 (6 - 7) sts at beg of
next 2 rows, 3 sts beg of next 4 (4 - 6) rows, 2
sts beg of next 4 (6 - 6) rows. Dec 1 st each
side every other row 1 (3 - 2) times—94 (96 -
102) sts rem. Work even until armhole measures 8¹⁄₂ (9 - 9¹⁄₂)″ / 21.5 (23 - 24) cm; end
WS row. *Next row (RS):* Work 23 (24 - 26) sts
for right shoulder and place on a holder; work
48 (48 - 50) sts for back neck and place on a
2nd holder; work rem sts for left shoulder and
place on a 3rd holder for later finishing.

FRONT

Work as for back until armhole measures ¹⁄₂
(1 - 1¹⁄₂)″ / .5 (2.5 - 4) cm, end with a WS row.
Shape armhole and neck: *Next row (RS):* Cont
armhole shaping as for back, and *at the same
time,* work to center, join 2nd ball of yarn, and
work to end. Working both sides at the same
time, dec 1 st at each neck edge every other
row 20 (20 - 22) times, then every 4th row 4
(4 - 3) times—23 (24 - 26) sts rem each side.
Work even until same length as back. Place
rem sts each side on holders.

SHOULDER SEAMS

For each shoulder, k seam tog as foll: Sl front
and back shoulder sts from holders to 2 dpns.
Hold pieces together with the wrong sides facing each other and sweater front facing you.

With a 3rd dpn, k first st from front needle tog with first st from back needle, *k next st from front and back needles tog, sl first st over 2nd st to bind off; rep from * until all sts are bound off. Cut yarn and pull end through loop.

FINISHING

Neckband: With RS facing and circular needle, k48 (48 - 50) sts from back neck holder, pick up and k52 (52 - 53) sts along left front neck, place marker, pick up 52 (52 - 53) sts along right front neck—152 (152 - 156) sts. Join and work in k1, p1 rib, dec 1 st each side of center marker every row until band measures 1″ / 2.5 cm. Bind off in rib. Sew side seams. **Armhole band:** With RS facing and circular needle, pick up and k118 (124 - 130) sts evenly around each armhole edge. Join and work in k1, p1 rib for 1″ / 2.5 cm. Bind off in rib.

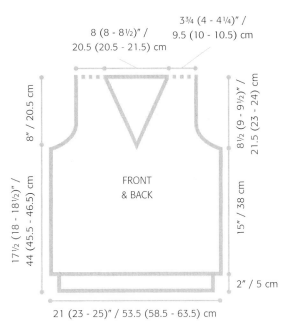

8 (8 - 8½)″ / 20.5 (20.5 - 21.5) cm

3¾ (4 - 4¼)″ / 9.5 (10 - 10.5) cm

8″ / 20.5 cm

8½ (9 - 9½)″ / 21.5 (23 - 24) cm

FRONT & BACK

17½ (18 - 18½)″ / 44 (45.5 - 46.5) cm

15″ / 38 cm

2″ / 5 cm

21 (23 - 25)″ / 53.5 (58.5 - 63.5) cm

Party Girl

Try this fabulously easy pullover; it's a great beginner project. Everyone from age two on up will love this design, timeless and elegant. Yarn choices make all the difference here; try different swatches to experiment. I love Chinchilla because it is lovely to wear and knit.

Simple Silhouette Pullover ■ Furry Chenille
Women's/Girl's ■ QuickKnit

SIZES

Child: 2 (4 - 6 - 8) years
Finished chest: 26 (28 - 30 - 32)" /
           66 (71 - 76 - 81) cm
Length, shoulder to hem: 12 (13 - 14 - 15)" /
           30 (33 - 35 - 38) cm

Adult: small (medium - large)
Finished chest: 40 (44 - 48)" / 101 (112 - 122) cm
Length, shoulder to hem: 20 (21 - 22)" /
           51 (53 - 56) cm

MATERIALS

Heavy weight chenille that will obtain gauge given below
Child: 230 (270 - 310 - 360) yd. / 210 (245 - 280 - 325) m
Adult: 600 (700 - 800) yd. / 540 (630 - 720) m
Knitting needles size 8 US (6 UK, 5 mm) or size needed to
    obtain gauge
Double pointed needles (dpns) size 8 US (6 UK, 5 mm)
Stitch holders
Samples in photographs knit in Berroco Chinchilla #5655
   Cool Red for child; #5370 Fire for adult

GAUGE

14 sts and 20 rows = 4" or 10 cm over St st using size 8 US (6 UK, 5 mm)
    needles
Always check gauge to save time and ensure correct yardage and correct fit!

Party Girl | Child

BACK

Cast on 47 (50 - 54 - 57) sts. Work in St st for 12 (13 - 14 - 15)" / 30 (33 - 35 - 38) cm or desired length to shoulder. Work 14 (15 - 17 - 17) sts and place on a holder for one shoulder, bind off next 19 (20 - 20 - 23) sts for back neck, work rem sts, and place on a 2nd holder for other shoulder.

FRONT

Work same as back until piece measures 10 (11 - 12 - 13)" / 25 (28 - 30 - 33) cm from beg or 2" / 5 cm less than length of back; end with a WS row. **Shape neck:** *Next row (RS):* K18 (19 - 21 - 21) sts, join 2nd ball of yarn and bind off center 11 (12 - 12 - 15) sts, k to end. Working both sides at same time, bind off from each neck edge 2 sts twice—14 (15 - 17 - 17) sts rem each side. Work even until piece measures same as back. Place rem sts on holders.

SHOULDER SEAMS

For each shoulder, k seam tog as foll: Sl front and back shoulder sts from holders to 2 dpns. Hold pieces together with wrong sides facing each other and sweater front facing you. With a 3rd dpn, k first st from front needle tog with first st from back needle, *k next st from front and back needles tog, sl first st over 2nd st to bind off; rep from * until all sts are bound off. Cut yarn and pull end through loop.

SLEEVES

Mark for sleeves 6 (6½ - 7 - 7½)" / 15 (16.5 - 17.5 - 19) cm down from shoulder seam on front and back. With RS facing, pick up and k42 (46 - 50 - 54) sts between markers. Work in St st as foll: Starting with a p row, work 5 rows even, then dec 1 st each end on next row, then every 6th row 4 (4 - 6 - 5) times more, every 4th row 3 (5 - 4 - 7) times—26 (26 - 28 - 28) sts rem. Work even until sleeve measures 9½ (11 - 12½ - 14)" / 24 (28 - 31.5 - 35.5) cm or desired length. Bind off loosely and evenly.

FINISHING
Sew side and sleeve seams.

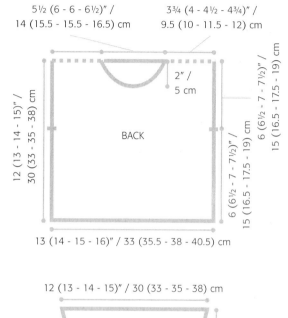

5½ (6 - 6 - 6½)" / 14 (15.5 - 15.5 - 16.5) cm

3¾ (4 - 4½ - 4¾)" / 9.5 (10 - 11.5 - 12) cm

6 (6½ - 7 - 7½)" / 15 (16.5 - 17.5 - 19) cm

2" / 5 cm

12 (13 - 14 - 15)" / 30 (33 - 35 - 38) cm

BACK

6 (6½ - 7 - 7½)" / 15 (16.5 - 17.5 - 19) cm

6 (6½ - 7 - 7½)" / 15 (16.5 - 17.5 - 19) cm

13 (14 - 15 - 16)" / 33 (35.5 - 38 - 40.5) cm

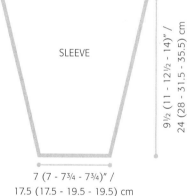

12 (13 - 14 - 15)" / 30 (33 - 35 - 38) cm

SLEEVE

9½ (11 - 12½ - 14)" / 24 (28 - 31.5 - 35.5) cm

7 (7 - 7¾ - 7¾)" / 17.5 (17.5 - 19.5 - 19.5) cm

Party Girl | Adult

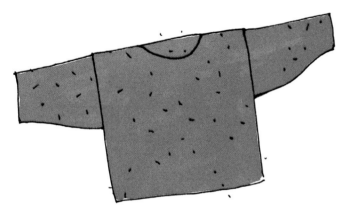

BACK

Cast on 72 (78 - 86) sts. Work in St st for 20 (21 - 22)″ / 51 (53 - 56) cm or desired length to shoulder. Work 22 (24 - 28) sts and place on a holder for one shoulder, bind off next 28 (30 - 30) sts for back neck, work rem sts, and place on a 2nd holder for other shoulder.

FRONT

Work same as back until piece measures 17 (18 - 19)″ / 43.5 (45.5 - 48.5) cm from beg or 3″ / 7.5 cm less than length of back; end with a

WS row. **Shape neck:** *Next row (RS):* K29 (31 - 35) sts, join 2nd ball of yarn and bind off center 14 (16 - 16) sts, k to end. Working both sides at same time, bind off from each neck edge 3 sts once, 1 st twice—14 (15 - 17 - 17) sts rem each side. Work even until piece measures same as back. Place rem sts on holders.

SHOULDER SEAMS

For each shoulder, k seam tog as foll: Sl front and back shoulder sts from holders to 2 dpns. Hold pieces together with wrong sides facing each other and sweater front facing you. With a 3rd dpn, k first st from front needle tog with first st from back needle, *k next st from front and back needles tog, sl first st over 2nd st to bind off; rep from * until all sts are bound off. Cut yarn and pull end through loop.

SLEEVES

Mark for sleeves 9 (9½ - 10)″ / 15 (16.5 - 17.5 - 19) cm down from shoulder seam on front and back. With RS facing, pick up and

k64 (68 - 72) sts between markers. Work in St
st as foll: Starting with a p row, work 5 rows
even, then dec 1 st each end on next row, then
every 6th row 12 (10 - 6) times more, every
4th row 3 (6 - 12) times—32 (34 - 34) sts rem.
Work even until sleeve measures 19″ / 48 cm
or desired length. Bind off loosely and evenly.

FINISHING
Sew side and sleeve seams.

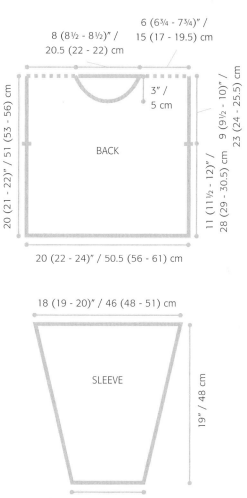

6 (6¾ - 7¾)″ /
15 (17 - 19.5) cm

8 (8½ - 8½)″ /
20.5 (22 - 22) cm

3″ /
5 cm

9 (9½ - 10)″ /
23 (24 - 25.5) cm

20 (21 - 22)″ / 51 (53 - 56) cm

BACK

11 (11½ - 12)″ /
28 (29 - 30.5) cm

20 (22 - 24)″ / 50.5 (56 - 61) cm

18 (19 - 20)″ / 46 (48 - 51) cm

SLEEVE

19″ / 48 cm

9 (9½ - 9½)″ / 23 (24 - 24) cm

It's your choice: sweater or vest. This pattern is simple and plain but a great sweater or vest in the right yarn. It is a basic for any wardrobe and a great beginner project.

Worsted Wool Pullover or Vest ▪ Unisex/Boy's ▪ QuickKnit

SIZES

Child: 8 (10 - 12 - 14) years
Finished chest: 34 (36 - 38 - 40)" /
              86 (91 - 96 - 101) cm
Length, shoulder to hem: 21 (22 - 23 - 24)" /
              53 (56 - 58 - 61) cm

Adult: small (medium - large)
Finished chest: 42 (46 - 50)" / 106 (117 - 127) cm
Length, shoulder to hem: 26 (26½ - 27)" /
              66 (67.5 - 68.5) cm

MATERIALS

Worsted weight wool that will obtain gauge given below
Child pullover: 665 (735 - 810 - 890) yd. / 600 (665 - 730 -
    800) m
Adult vest: 675 (755 - 835) yd. / 610 (680 - 755) m
Knitting needles size 8 US (6 UK, 5 mm) or size needed to
    obtain gauge
Double pointed needles (dpns) size 8 US (6 UK, 5 mm)
16" / 40 cm circular needle size 8 US (6 UK, 5 mm)
Stitch holders
Samples in photographs knit in Berroco Wensleydale #154
    Aubergine for child; #151 Taupe for adult

GAUGE

19 sts and 25 rows = 4" or 10 cm over St st using size 8 US (6 UK,
    5 mm) needles
Always check gauge to save time and ensure correct yardage and correct fit!

Crew Pullover | Child

BACK

Cast on 81 (86 - 90 - 96) sts. Work in k1, p1 rib for 1" / 2.5 cm. Cont in St st until piece measures 21 (22 - 23 - 24)" / 53 (56 - 58 - 61) cm or desired length to shoulder. *Next row:* Work 24 (25 - 27 - 29) sts for one shoulder and place on a holder; bind off 33 (36 - 36 - 38) sts for back neck; work rem sts, and place on a 2nd holder for other shoulder.

FRONT

Work as for back until piece measures 18 (19 - 20 - 21)" / 45.5 (48.5 - 50.5 - 53.5) cm from beg, or 3" / 7.5 cm less than length of back;

end with a WS row. **Shape neck:** *Next row (RS):* Work 34 (35 - 37 - 39) sts, join 2nd ball of yarn and bind off center 13 (16 - 16 - 18) sts; work to end. Working both sides at same time, bind off from each neck edge 3 sts once, 2 sts twice, dec 1 st every other row 3 times— 24 (25 - 27 - 29) sts rem each side. Work even until same length as back. Place rem sts on holder.

SHOULDER SEAMS

For each shoulder, k seam tog as foll: Sl front and back shoulder sts from holders to 2 dpns. Hold pieces together with wrong sides facing each other and sweater front facing you. With a 3rd dpn, k first st from front needle tog with first st from back needle, *k next st from front and back needles tog, sl first st over 2nd st to bind off; rep from * until all sts are bound off. Cut yarn and pull end through loop.

SLEEVES

Mark for sleeves 8½ (9 - 9½ - 10)" / 21.5 (23 - 24 - 25.5) cm down from shoulder seam on front and back. With RS facing, pick up and k80 (86 - 90 - 96) sts between markers. Work in St st as foll: Work 3 (5 - 5 - 7) rows even, then dec 1 st each end on next row, then every 4th row 18 (19 - 21 - 23) times more—42 (46 - 46 - 48) sts rem. Work even until sleeve measures 13 (14 - 15½ - 17)" / 33 (35.5 - 39.5 - 43) cm. Work in k1, p1 rib for 1" / 2.5 cm. Bind off loosely and evenly in rib.

FINISHING

Sew side and sleeve seams. **Neckband:** With RS facing and circular needle, pick up and k approx 62 (68 - 68 - 72) sts evenly around neck edge. Join and work in k1, p1 rib for 1" / 2.5 cm. Bind off loosely in rib.

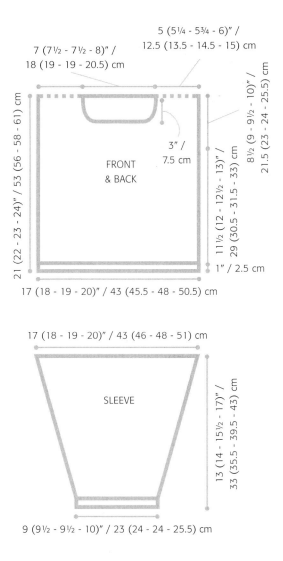

Crew Vest | Adult

BACK

Cast on 100 (110 - 118) sts. Work in k1, p1 rib for 1" / 2.5 cm. Cont in St st until piece measures 16½" / 42 cm from beg or desired length to armhole; end with a WS row. **Shape armhole:** Bind off 3 sts at beg of next 2 (4 - 4) rows. Dec 1 st each side on next row, then every other row 8 (8 - 9) times more—76 (80 - 86) sts rem. Work even until armhole measures 9½ (10 - 10½)" / 24 (25.5 - 26.5) cm. Work 19 (20 - 22) sts for one shoulder and place on a holder; bind off next 38 (40 - 42) sts for back neck; work rem sts and place on a 2nd holder for other shoulder.

FRONT

Work as for back until armhole measures 6½ (7 - 7½)" / 16.5 (18 - 19) cm; end with a WS row. **Shape neck:** *Next row (RS):* K28 (29 - 31) sts, join 2nd ball of yarn and bind off center 20 (22 - 24) sts, k to end. Working both sides at same time, bind off from each neck edge 3 sts once, 2 sts twice, dec 1 st every other row twice—19 (20 - 22) sts rem each side. Work even until same length as back. Place rem sts on holders.

SHOULDER SEAMS

For each shoulder, k seam tog as foll: Sl front and back shoulder sts from holders to 2 dpns. Hold pieces together with wrong sides facing each other and sweater front facing you. With a 3rd dpn, k first st from front needle tog with first st from back needle, *k next st from front and back needles tog, sl first st over 2nd st to bind off; rep from * until all sts are bound off. Cut yarn and pull end through loop.

FINISHING

Sew side and sleeve seams. **Neckband:** With RS facing and circular needle, pick up and k74 (78 - 86) sts evenly around neck edge. Join and work in k1, p1 rib for 1" / 2.5 cm. Bind off in rib. **Armhole band:** With RS facing and circular needle, pick up and k94 (100 - 106) sts evenly around each armhole edge. Join and work in k1, p1 rib for 1" / 2.5 cm. Bind off in rib.

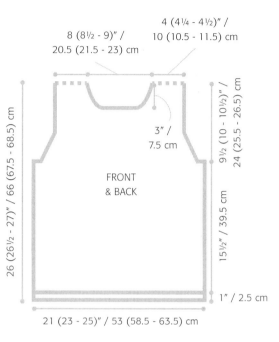

4 (4¼ - 4½)" /
10 (10.5 - 11.5) cm

8 (8½ - 9)" /
20.5 (21.5 - 23) cm

9½ (10 - 10½)" /
24 (25.5 - 26.5) cm

3" /
7.5 cm

FRONT
& BACK

26 (26½ - 27)" / 66 (67.5 - 68.5) cm

15½" / 39.5 cm

1" / 2.5 cm

21 (23 - 25)" / 53 (58.5 - 63.5) cm

Bow Tie

After knitting this Chanel-style cardigan, you simply cut lengths of ribbon, pull the ribbon through a few stitches, and tie a single knot. Trim the ribbon, and you have bows like butterflies trimming your sweater. This is definitely a party piece!

Cropped Cardigan with Ribbon Ties ▪ Women's/Girl's ▪ QuickKnit

SIZES

Child: 2 (4 - 6 - 8) years
Finished chest (buttoned): 28 (30 - 32 - 34)" /
$\qquad$ 71 (76.5 - 81 - 86.5) cm
Length, shoulder to hem: 14 (15 - 16 - 17)" /
$\qquad$ 35.5 (38 - 40.5 - 43.5) cm

Adult: small (medium - large)
Finished bust (buttoned): 38 (42 - 46)" / 96.5 (106.5 - 117) cm
Length, shoulder to hem: 18½ (19½ - 20)" / 47 (49.5 - 51) cm

MATERIALS

Aran weight yarn that will obtain gauge given below
Child: 275 (325 - 380 - 445) yd. / 247 (292 - 342 - 400) m
Adult: 560 (620 - 710) yd. / 504 (560 - 640) m
Knitting needles sizes 7 and 9 US (7 and 5 UK, 4.5 and 5.5 mm)
$\quad$ or size needed to obtain gauge
Double pointed needles (dpns) size 9 US (5 UK, 5.5 mm)
Crochet hook size K / 10.5 US (3 UK, 7 mm) for attaching
$\quad$ bows
Stitch holders
4 buttons for child; 5 buttons for adult
1 yd. / 1 m of 1½" / 4 cm wide nylon ribbon
Samples in photographs knit in Berroco Mohair Classic #B1110 Purple

GAUGE

16 sts and 20 rows = 4" or 10 cm over St st using larger needles
Always check gauge to save time and ensure correct yardage and correct fit!

Bow Tie | Child

Seed St

Row 1 (RS): *K1, p1; rep from * to end.
Row 2: K the p sts and p the k sts.
Rep row 2 for seed st.

BACK

With smaller needles, cast on 58 (62 - 66 - 70) sts. Work in seed st for 1″ / 2.5 cm, end with a WS row. Change to larger needles and, starting with a k row, work in St st until piece measures 14 (15 - 16 - 17)″ / 35.5 (38 - 40.5 - 43.5) cm from beg or desired length to shoulder. Work 18 (19 - 20 - 22) sts and place on a holder for one shoulder; bind off next 22 (24 - 26 - 26) sts for back neck; work rem sts and place on a 2nd holder for other shoulder.

LEFT FRONT

With smaller needles, cast on 31 (33 - 35 - 37) sts. Work in seed st for 1″ / 2.5 cm, end with a WS row. Change to larger needles. *Next row (RS):* K27 (29 - 31 - 33), work last 4 sts in seed

st for buttonband. Cont in St st, keeping 4 buttonband sts in seed st until piece measures 12 (13 - 14 - 15)″ / 30.5 (33 - 35.5 - 38.5) cm from beg or 2″ / 5 cm less than length of back; end with a WS row. **Shape neck:** *Next row (RS):* K to last 4 sts, place rem 4 sts on a holder. *Next row:* Bind off 3 sts, p to end. Cont to bind off 3 sts beg of WS rows 0 (1 - 2 - 2) time more, then 2 sts 3 (2 - 1 - 1) times—18 (19 - 20 - 22) sts rem. Work even until same length as back. Place rem sts on a holder. Place markers on buttonband for 4 buttons, first one just above seed st edging, last one 1″ / .5 cm below neck shaping and 2 others spaced evenly between.

RIGHT FRONT

Cast on and work edging as for left front. Change to larger needles. *Next row (RS):* **Buttonhole row:** Seed 2, yo, k2tog, k27 (29 - 31 - 33) sts. Cont in St st, keeping 4 buttonhole band sts in seed st and working buttonhole opposite each marker. Work until piece measures same as left front to neck, end with a RS row. **Shape neck:** *Next row (WS):* P to last 4 sts, sl last 4 sts to holder. *Next row:* Bind off 3 sts, k to end. Cont to work neck shaping beg of RS rows as for left front. Work even until same length as back. Place rem sts on a holder.

SHOULDER SEAMS

For each shoulder, k seam tog as foll: Sl front and back shoulder sts from holders to 2 dpns. Hold pieces together with wrong sides facing each other and sweater front facing you. With a 3rd dpn, k first st from front needle tog with

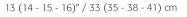

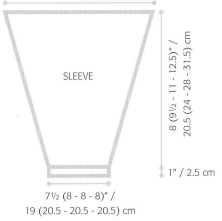

13 (14 - 15 - 16)" / 33 (35 - 38 - 41) cm

SLEEVE

8 (9½ - 11 - 12.5)" / 20.5 (24 - 28 - 31.5) cm

1" / 2.5 cm

7½ (8 - 8 - 8)" / 19 (20.5 - 20.5 - 20.5) cm

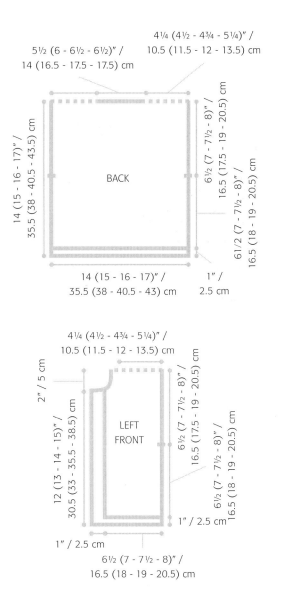

5½ (6 - 6½ - 6½)" / 14 (16.5 - 17.5 - 17.5) cm

4¼ (4½ - 4¾ - 5¼)" / 10.5 (11.5 - 12 - 13.5) cm

BACK

14 (15 - 16 - 17)" / 35.5 (38 - 40.5 - 43.5) cm

6½ (7 - 7½ - 8)" / 16.5 (17.5 - 19 - 20.5) cm

6½ (7 - 7½ - 8)" / 16.5 (18 - 19 - 20.5) cm

14 (15 - 16 - 17)" / 35.5 (38 - 40.5 - 43) cm

1" / 2.5 cm

4¼ (4½ - 4¾ - 5¼)" / 10.5 (11.5 - 12 - 13.5) cm

2" / 5 cm

LEFT FRONT

12 (13 - 14 - 15)" / 30.5 (33 - 35.5 - 38.5) cm

6½ (7 - 7½ - 8)" / 16.5 (17.5 - 19 - 20.5) cm

6½ (7 - 7½ - 8)" / 16.5 (18 - 19 - 20.5) cm

1" / 2.5 cm

1" / 2.5 cm

6½ (7 - 7½ - 8)" / 16.5 (18 - 19 - 20.5) cm

first st from back needle, *k next st from front and back needles tog, sl first st over 2nd st to bind off; rep from * until all sts are bound off. Cut yarn and pull end through loop.

SLEEVES

Mark for sleeves 6½ (7 - 7½ - 8)" / 16.5 (17.5 - 19 - 20.5) cm down from shoulder seam on front and back. With RS facing, pick up and k54 (58 - 62 - 66) sts between markers. Working in St st starting with a p row, work 3 rows even. Dec 1 st each end on next row, then every 4th row 5 (8 - 9 - 11) times more, then every 2nd row 6 (4 - 5 - 5) times—30 (32 - 32 - 32) sts rem. Work even until sleeve measures 8 (9½ - 11 - 12½)" / 20.5 (24 - 28 - 31.5) cm or 1" / 2.5 cm less than desired length. Change to smaller needles and work in seed st for 1" / 2.5 cm. Bind off loosely and evenly in seed st.

FINISHING

Neckband: With RS facing and smaller needles, work 4 sts in seed st from right front holder, pick up and k11 (12 - 13 - 13) sts along right front neck, 16 (18 - 20 - 20) sts along back neck, 11 (12 - 13 - 13) sts along

left front neck, work rem 4 sts from left front holder in seed st—46 (50 - 54 - 54) sts. Work in rev St st for 3 rows. Bind off purlwise. Sew side and sleeve seams. Sew on buttons. Cut ribbon approx 6" / 15.5 cm long, cutting ends on a diagonal. With crochet hook, pull ribbon through 2 sts and tie. Trim to desired length.

Bow Tie | Adult

Seed St

Row 1 (RS): *K1, p1; rep from * to end.
Row 2: K the p sts and p the k sts.
Rep row 2 for seed st.

BACK

With smaller needles, cast on 78 (86 - 94) sts. Work in seed st for 1" / 2.5 cm; end with a WS row. Change to larger needles and, starting with a k row, work in St st until piece measures 18 (19 - 20)" / 47 (49.5 - 51) cm from beg, or desired length to shoulder. Work 27 (30 - 33) sts and place on a holder for one shoulder; bind off next 24 (26 - 28) sts for back neck; work rem sts and place on a 2nd holder for other shoulder.

LEFT FRONT

With smaller needles, cast on 42 (46 - 50) sts. Work in seed st for 1" / 2.5 cm; end with a WS row. Change to larger needles. *Next row (RS):* K36 (40 - 44), work last 6 sts in seed st for

buttonband. Cont in St st, keeping 6 buttonband sts in seed st until piece measures 16 (17 - 17½)" / 40.5 (43 - 44) cm from beg or 2½" / 6 cm less than length of back; end with a WS row. **Shape neck:** *Next row (RS):* K to last 6 sts, place rem 6 sts on a holder. *Next row:* Bind off 3 sts, p to end. Cont to bind off 3 sts beg of WS rows 0 (1 - 2) times more, then 2 sts 3 (2 - 1) times—27 (30 - 33) sts rem. Work even until same length as back. Place rem sts on a holder. Place markers on buttonband for 5 buttons, first one just above seed st edging, last one 1" / .5 cm below neck shaping, and 3 others spaced evenly between.

RIGHT FRONT

Cast on and work edging as for left front. Change to larger needles. *Next row (RS):* **Buttonhole row:** Seed 2, yo, k2tog, seed 2, k36 (40 - 44) sts. Cont in St st, keeping 6 buttonhole band sts in seed st and working buttonhole opposite each marker. Work until piece measures same as left front to neck; end with a RS row. **Shape neck:** *Next row (WS):* P to last 6 sts, sl last 6 sts to holder. *Next row:* Bind off 3 sts, k to end. Cont to work neck, shaping beg of RS rows as for left front. Work even until same length as back. Place rem sts on a holder.

SHOULDER SEAMS

For each shoulder, k seam tog as foll: Sl front and back shoulder sts from holders to 2 dpns. Hold pieces together with wrong sides facing each other and sweater front facing you. With

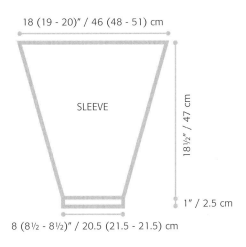

18 (19 - 20)" / 46 (48 - 51) cm

SLEEVE

18½" / 47 cm

1" / 2.5 cm

8 (8½ - 8½)" / 20.5 (21.5 - 21.5) cm

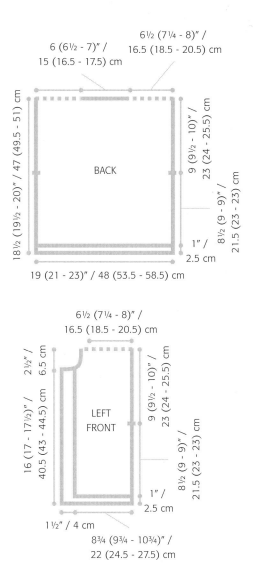

6½ (7¼ - 8)" /
16.5 (18.5 - 20.5) cm

6 (6½ - 7)" /
15 (16.5 - 17.5) cm

BACK

18½ (19½ - 20)" / 47 (49.5 - 51) cm

9 (9½ - 10)" /
23 (24 - 25.5) cm

8½ (9 - 9)" /
21.5 (23 - 23) cm

1" /
2.5 cm

19 (21 - 23)" / 48 (53.5 - 58.5) cm

6½ (7¼ - 8)" /
16.5 (18.5 - 20.5) cm

2½" /
6.5 cm

16 (17 - 17½)" /
40.5 (43 - 44.5) cm

LEFT
FRONT

9 (9½ - 10)" /
23 (24 - 25.5) cm

8½ (9 - 9)" /
21.5 (23 - 23) cm

1" /
2.5 cm

1½" / 4 cm

8¾ (9¾ - 10¾)" /
22 (24.5 - 27.5) cm

a 3rd dpn, k first st from front needle tog with first st from back needle, *k next st from front and back needles tog, sl first st over 2nd st to bind off; rep from * until all sts are bound off. Cut yarn and pull end through loop.

SLEEVES
Mark for sleeves 9 (9½ - 10)" / 23 (24 - 25.5) cm down from shoulder seam on front and back. With RS facing, pick up and k74 (78 - 82) sts between markers. Working in St st starting with a p row, work 5 rows even. Dec 1 st each end on next row, then every 6th row 2 (0 - 0) times more, then every 4th row 17 (20 - 18) times, then every 2nd row 0 (0 - 4) times—34 (36 - 36) sts rem. Work even until sleeve measures 18½" / 47 cm or 1" / 2.5 cm less than desired length. Change to smaller needles and work in seed st for 1" / 2.5 cm. Bind off loosely and evenly in seed st.

FINISHING
Neckband: With RS facing and smaller needles, work 6 sts in seed st from right front holder, pick up and k14 (15 - 16) sts along

right front neck, 24 (26 - 28) sts along back neck, 14 (15 - 16) sts along left front neck, work rem 6 sts from left front holder in seed st—64 (68 - 72) sts. Work in rev St st for 3 rows. Bind off purlwise. Sew side and sleeve seams. Sew on buttons. Cut ribbon approx 6" / 15.5 cm long, cutting ends on a diagonal. With crochet hook, pull ribbon through 2 sts and tie. Trim to desired length.

Etc!

Accessories galore, knit in a jiffy, warm to wear, great for presents and for learning to knit!

Twizzler

Like my earlier Twizzle Tops, this bulky weight topper is knit from the top down using five double pointed needles. A bit pokey at first, this hat knits very quickly in one color; it takes me about two hours. The soutache trim is a single crochet chain, sewn on later and embellished with French knot bobbles.

Chapeau with Soutache and Bobble Trim ▪ Unisex ▪ QuickKnit

SIZES

Child's medium (adult's small)
Circumference: 20″ / 50.5 cm
Note: After I-cord border, finished circumference is approx
3″ / 7.5 cm smaller

MATERIALS

Worsted weight mohair or wool used double stranded
100 (150) yd. / 90 (135) m (MC)
Small amounts in 2 contrasting colors A and B
Knitting needles, 1 set (5) double pointed (dp) size 11 US
(0 UK, 8 mm) or size needed to obtain gauge
Knitting needles size 9 US (5 UK, 5.5 mm) for bobbles
Crochet hook size I / 9 US (5 UK, 5.5 mm) for swirls
Stitch holder
Samples in photographs knit in Berroco Mohair Classic

GAUGE

12 sts and 20 rows = 4″ or 10 cm over St st using 2 strands held tog
Always check gauge to save time and ensure correct yardage and correct fit!

Twizzler | Child and Adult

TWIZZLE TOP

With 2 strands MC held tog, cast on 4 sts. Work I-cord as foll: K4, *do not turn work. Slide sts to other end of needle to work next row from RS and k4; rep from * for 1" / 2.5 cm.

HAT

Inc 1 st in each st on next row—8 sts. Divide sts evenly over 4 dpns (2 sts on each needle). Working in rnds of St st (k every rnd), inc 1 st at end of each needle every rnd (therefore 4 sts increased every rnd) until there are 60 (72) sts, or 15 (18) sts on each needle. **Note:** To make hat smaller or larger, work fewer or more inc rnds. For turning ridge, k1 rnd, p4 rnds. Cont

to k every rnd for 2 (3)" / 5 (7.5) cm, or desired depth. Leave sts on 3 needles. Place st from 4th needle on holder.

I-CORD BORDER

Leave sts on 3 dpns, placing sts from 1 dpn on holder or piece of yarn. With 2 dpns and MC, cast on 4 sts and work I-cord as before, attaching cord to lower edge of hat, with right side facing, as foll: *K last st of I-cord tog with 1 st from hat* through back loop. Rep from * until no sts rem. Bind off last 4 sts, and sew I-cord ends tog.

CHAIN SWIRLS

With crochet hook and double strand of A, chain approx 40" / 102 cm. Do not fasten off. Sew chain to border of hat, forming swirls and loops (see photo for inspiration), adjusting length of chain if necessary. Make 6 bobbles as foll: With smaller needles and double strand of B, cast on 2 sts. *Row 1:* K1, inc in next st—3 sts. *Row 2:* P3 sts. *Row 3:* K2tog, k1. *Row 4:* P2tog. Cut yarn, leaving long tail, and pull through loop. Sew bobbles to border as shown in the drawings above.

Pipi Boot Stockings

Knitters in my classes always knit these and usually keep the first pair for themselves. Warm and light, soft and thick, these sox are wonderful under boots or clogs. A perfect gift, too. And yes, turning the heel couldn't be easier; just slow down and read the instructions, and it's done before you know it!

Bulky Boot Sox ▪ Unisex ▪ QuickKnit

SIZES

Child (woman, man)

MATERIALS

Bulky weight wool that will obtain gauge given
    below
100 (200 - 220) yd. / 90 (180 - 200) m
For all sizes: double pointed needles (dpns) size
    8 US (6 UK, 5 mm) or size needed to obtain
    gauge
For child's and woman's sizes only: Dpns size 6
    US (8 UK, 4 mm)
*Samples in photographs knit in JCA Reynolds
    Andean Alpaca Regal*

GAUGE

18 sts and 24 rows = 4″ or 10 cm over St st
    using size 8 US (6 UK, 5 mm) needles
Always check gauge to save time and ensure correct yardage and correct fit!

Pipi Boot Stockings | Child and Adult

STOCKING TOP

With larger dpns, cast on 32 (40) sts, and distribute on 3 needles as foll: 12 - 10 - 10 (12 - 14 - 14). Join, being careful not to twist sts. Work in k1, p1 rib for 4 (6)″ / 10 (15.5) cm.

HEEL FLAP

Rearrange sts on 3 needles as foll: 16 - 8 - 8 (20 - 10 - 10). Working back and forth on the 16 (20) sts for the heel flap, work as foll: *Next row (RS):* *K1, sl 1; rep from *; end k2. *Next row:* P. Repeat these 2 rows until heel measures 1 (2)″ / 2.5 (5) cm, ending with a RS row.

TURNING HEEL

Row 1 (WS): P10 (12), p2tog, p1, turn work.
Row 2: Sl 1 st, k5, k2tog, k1, turn.
Row 3: Sl 1, p6, p2tog, p1, turn.
Row 4: Sl 1, k7, k2tog, k1, turn.
Row 5: Sl 1, p8, p2tog, p0 (1), turn.

Child's
Row 6: Sl 1, k8, k2tog—10 sts rem.

Adult's
Row 6: Sl 1, k9, k2tog, k1.
Row 7: Sl 1, p10, p2tog, turn.
Row 8: Sl 1, k10, k2tog—12 sts rem.

GUSSET

With RS of heel flap facing and same needle, pick up and k8 (10) sts along left side of heel flap (needle 1), k next 16 (20) sts for instep (needle 2), pick up and k8 (10) sts along right side of heel flap and k5 (6) sts from heel (needle 3), k rem 5 (6) sts from heel onto needle 1—13 (16) sts on needles 1 and 3 and 16 (20) sts on needle 2. Work dec rnd as foll: *Needle 1:* K to last 3 sts, k2tog, k1. *Needle 2:* K. *Needle 3:* K1, k2tog, k rem sts. Rep dec rnd every other rnd a total of 5 (6) times—8 - 16 - 8 (10 - 20 - 10) sts.

STOCKING FOOT

For child's and woman's sizes, change to smaller size dpns. K in rnds until sock measures 2 (3)″ / 5 (7.5) cm less than desired length. Work dec rnd as foll: *Needle 1:* K to last 3 sts, k2tog, k1. *Needle 2:* K1, k2tog, k to last 3 sts, k2tog, k1. *Needle 3:* k1, k2tog, k rem sts. K3 (4) rnds. Rep dec rnd. K2 (3) rnds. Rep dec rnd. K1 (2) rnds. Rep dec rnd. K1 rnd.

Rep dec rnd. K0 (1) rnd. [Rep dec rnd] 0 (2) times—6 sts on front needle, 3 sts on 2 back needles. Sl sts from 2 back needles to a single needle—6 sts rem each needle.

FINISHING
Weave the last sts tog using kitchener st.

KITCHENER STITCH
1. Bring yarn needle though front st as if to p, leaving st on needle.

2. Bring yarn needle through back st as if to k, leaving st on needle.
3. Bring yarn needle through same front st as if to k, and then slip this st off needle. Bring yarn needle through next front st as if to p, again leaving st on needle.
4. Bring yarn needle through first back st as if to p, slip st off, and then bring yarn needle through next back st as if to k, leaving it on needle. Rep steps 3 and 4 until all sts are used up.

Thumbs Up

Made on 26 stitches on two needles, these mittens have become the staple of my beginning knitting classes. This pattern was inspired by one of my knitters, Jane Howard, who gave me a mitten pattern for two strands of worsted wool worked together in this type of format. Adapted, one ball of Lopi makes two mitts, and oh, those fabulous colors!

Big Cabled Mittens on 2 Needles ▪ Unisex ▪ QuickKnit

SIZES

Child (woman, man)

MATERIALS

Bulky weight wool that will obtain gauge given below
100 (110 - 120) yd. / 90 (100 - 110) m
Knitting needles size 10 US (4 UK, 6 mm) or size needed to obtain gauge
Cable needle (cn)
Samples in photographs knit in JCA Reynolds Lopi

GAUGE

14 sts = 4″ or 10 cm over St st
Always check gauge to save time and ensure correct yardage and correct fit!

Thumbs Up | Child and Adult

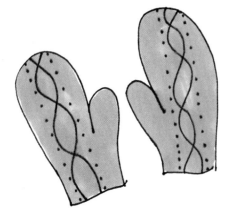

Cable Panel (over 10 sts)

Rows 1, 3, 5, and 7 (WS): K2, p6, k2.

Rows 2, 6, and 8: P2, k6, p2.

Row 4: P2, sl next 3 sts to cn and hold to
    back of work, k3, k3 from cn, p2.

Rep rows 1–8 for cable panel.

RIGHT MITTEN

Cast on 22 (26 - 30) sts. Work in St st and
cable panel as foll: *Next row (WS):* P10 (14 -
16), work row 1 of cable panel over next 10
sts, p2 (2- 4). Cont in St st and cable pat as est
for 2 (3 - 3½)" / 6.5 (7.5 - 9) cm; end with a
WS row.

THUMB GORE

Next row (RS) inc row: Keeping to pat, work
13 (14 - 16) sts, place marker, inc in next st,
k1, inc in next st, place marker, k6 (9 - 11) sts.

Cont to work in pats as est, rep inc row every
RS row until there are 9 (9 - 11) sts between
markers; end WS row. *Next row (RS):* Work
13 (14 - 16) sts and place on a holder, k9 (9 -
11) and leave on needle, place rem 6 (9 - 11)
sts on a holder.

THUMB

Cont on thumb sts only as foll: *Next row
(WS):* Cast on 0 (1 - 1) st, k9 (9 - 11), cast on
0 (1 - 1) st—9 (11 - 13) sts. Work even in St st
for 8 (10 - 12) rows. *Next row (RS):* K1,
*k2tog; rep from * across row. Cut yarn and
pull through rem sts. Sew thumb seam.

HAND

Place sts from first holder onto needle, pick up
and k3 sts across thumb gusset, work sts from
2nd holder—22 (26 - 30) sts. Cont in St st and
cable pat until hand measures 3 (3¾ - 4)" / 7.5
(9.5 - 10) cm above thumb; end with a WS row.

TOP SHAPING

Row 1 (RS): K2 (2 - 4), p2tog, k6, p2tog, k0
    (4 - 4), k2tog, k4, sl 1, k1, psso, k2 (2 -
    4)—18 (22 - 26) sts rem.

Rows 2 and 4: K all k sts, p all p sts.

Row 3: K2 (2 - 4), k2tog, k2, k2tog, k0 (4 - 4),
    k2tog, k4, sl 1, k1, psso, k2 (2 - 4)—14
    (18 - 22) sts rem.

Row 5: *K2tog; rep from * across—7 (9 - 11)
    sts rem.

Cut yarn, pull through rem sts, and sew back seam. Weave in all loose ends.

LEFT MITTEN
Cast on 22 (26 - 30) sts and reverse pat as foll: *Row 1 (WS):* P2 (2 - 4), work cable panel over next 10 sts, p10 (14 - 16). Work as for right mitten to thumb gore. *Next row (RS) inc row:* Keeping to pat, k6 (9 - 11) sts, place marker, inc in next st, k1, inc in next st, place marker, work 13 (14 - 16) sts. Complete as for right mitten.

Mo-Mitts

Worked on two needles, this mitten is knit in delicious mohair. Warm, light, and a bit dressy as mittens go, this is perfect for beginners.

SIZES

Child (adult)

MATERIALS

Worsted weight mohair used double stranded to
    obtain gauge given below
90 (160) yd. / 80 (145) m
Knitting needles, one pair straight size 6 and 8 US
    (8 and 6 UK, 4 and 8 mm) or size needed to
    obtain gauge
Stitch markers
Samples knit in Berroco Classic Mohair

GAUGE

14 sts = 4″ / 10 cm over St st using double stranded
    mohair
*Always check gauge to save time and ensure correct
    yardage and correct fit!*

Mo-Mitts | Child and Adult

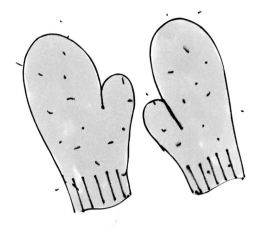

CUFF

With smaller needles, cast on 24 (28) sts. Work in k1, p1 rib for 2 (3)″ / 5 (7.5) cm, end with RS row, inc 3 (5) sts evenly across last row—27 (33) sts. Change to larger needles and, starting with a p row, work even in St st for 0 (4) row. *Next row (WS):* P12 (15) sts, place marker, p 3 sts, place marker, p rem sts.

THUMB GORE

Next row (RS) inc row: K, inc in st after first marker and last st before 2nd marker. Cont in St st, working inc row every other row until you have 9 (11) sts between markers; end with a RS row.

THUMB

Next row (WS): Work 12 (15) sts and place on holder; work 9 (11) thumb sts; work rem sts and place on holder. Cut yarn. Join yarn and cont to work thumb sts only for 1 (2)″ / 2.5 (5) cm; end WS row. K1, *k2tog; rep from * across next row, cut yarn, and pull through rem sts. Sew thumb seam and turn right side out.

HAND

With RS facing, k12 (15) sts from holder, pick up 3 sts across thumb, k rem sts from holder—27 (33) sts. Work even until mitten measures 6 (10)″ / 15 (25) cm from beg; end WS row. *Next row, dec row:* K1, *k2tog; rep from * across. *Next row:* Rep last 2 rows 2 more times. Cut yarn and pull through rem sts. Sew side seam.

ChinChilly

A beginner's dream, this garter stitch strip is sewn together to make a warm and fuzzy neckwarmer— also lovely done in bulky alpaca! It's great for the ski slopes or the city street; you'll want to whip up a batch for everyone you love.

Chenille Neckwarmer ■ Unisex ■ QuickKnit

SIZES

Child (adult)

MATERIALS

Chunky weight yarn that will obtain gauge given below
65 (105) yd. / 60 (95) m
Needles 9 US (5 UK, 5.5 mm) or size needed to obtain
    gauge
Samples in photographs knit in Berocco Chinchilla

GAUGE

16 sts = 4" / 10 cm over garter st
*Always check gauge to save time and ensure correct
    yardage and correct fit!*

Cast on 24 (32) sts. Work in garter st
(k all rows) until piece measures 18
(24)" / 45 (60) cm. Bind off. Sew the
short ends together.
Voila!

Merci!

A book like this one is an enormous endeavor above and beyond the design. Production for this book was accomplished over a series of many months, in a swirl of creative energy. Making schedules and scouting talent and locations, organizing photo shoots and finding props, shopping for perfect accessories, making panicked phone calls for a stand-in model for a no-show . . . it all continued for months!

I can design all day, but I can never match the extraordinary work of my dedicated and talented knitters. I could never even begin to

write patterns with the clarity, simplicity, and accuracy of Carla Scott. Judith Shangold outshines me with her eagle-eye pattern proofing and editing. I could never, even on a clear and sparkling day with perfect light, capture the beauty and charisma of my models as Nina Fuller does. I could never charm a child; curl the hair; and fix the innumerable, infinitesimal details that catch the eye of my stylist Merle Hagelin. And as for sets and locations and props, Isabel Smiles's deft and talented touch is everywhere. Enormous thanks to you all!

ABOUT JIL ET AL.

After a multifaceted education in art at Skidmore College, Colby College, and the Graduate School of Design at Harvard University, **Jil Eaton**'s professional career as painter, graphic designer, arts administrator, and restaurateur has dressed her in many hats, most lately as an internationally acclaimed knitwear designer. She designs, publishes, and distributes internationally an independent line of hand-knitting patterns for children's wear under the MinnowKnits label. A formidable knitter, Jil Eaton creates designs that have a comfortable but chic silhouette, encompassing both the traditional and the newest trends, adapting everything in easy-to-knit projects with great attention to detail, fresh styling, and unusual colorways. Fascinated with color and fashion, Jil's inspiration comes from many diverse directions, from the pages of French *Vogue* to paintings in the Met. Never at a loss for ideas, Jil produces two collections annually, designs for *Vogue Knitting International* and other publications, and is busy with her fourth book. Always

returning to her deep-seated love of knitting, designing knitwear focuses all her talents. Her spacious studios are clean and white, full of sketches, drawings, photographs, and mountains of delicious yarns. Jil juggles work for the collections, travel, and life with her financier husband David; her son Alexander; and an enormous, sleek black dog. And in spite of all the deadlines and responsibilities inherent in such a busy life, she still loves to knit!

Nina Van Brocklyn Fuller is the one who so deftly captures all these charming models on film. A nationally acclaimed location and studio photographer, Nina has degrees from Silvermine College of Art and George Washington University in photography, painting, and printmaking. After college, Nina worked the big time in New York City, assisting the talented stock photographer Nancy Brown, and shooting, shooting, shooting. Always on her toes, always with a camera in hand, Nina has a gift for catching the right angle, finding the most beautiful light, capturing the exact moment when the tear falls or the smile breaks. Location photography has emerged as a creative focus for Nina, and her major clients include L.L. Bean, Lands' End,

Atlantic Records, and last, but not least, MinnowKnits International. Her on-the-spot location work with people is rarely matched, as her inimitable charm and energy transfix her beguiled subjects.

Nina lives in Maine with her two beautiful children, whom we often see through her camera lens in this book. Growing up in the studio, constantly in front of one camera or another, both kids have a presence and inner light that are remarkably tangible. As does Nina.

After years of fashion and retail experience, **Merle Hagelin** decided to change her direction, and we're delighted she did. In beauty school for about 10 minutes, Merle drew instead on her many natural talents and instantly made quite a splash as a makeup artist in film and video. Her first makeup assignment was with Joe Brennan, the governor of the state of Maine, and this became a springboard into a career filled with interesting personalities. She has used her magic wands on President George Bush, baseball icon Ted Williams, *LA Law*'s Richard Dysart, wild and scary author Stephen King, and even the revered Martha Stewart!

Her prestigious national and international clients include L.L. Bean, Coca-Cola, NBC, CBS, AT&T, Atlantic Records, Bose Industries, Digital, and of course MinnowKnits International. Merle can finesse any situation, gets nervous models to breathe and light up, and makes even the scruffiest curmudgeon beautiful. With her magic touch and smile, Merle is the best baby wrangler on the planet.

Isabel Smiles is my design sounding board as well as location stylist. She moved to Maine 10 years ago, after a successful run as a stylist and antiques and design shop owner in New York and Connecticut, and created the world-renowned Pomegranate Inn Bed and Breakfast, a stunning small hotel in Portland, Maine. We have shot some of this book in her landmark inn; and her wonderful rich rooms full of art, antiques, hand-painted wall treatments, and other remarkable details, all put together with her unbelievably talented eye, have created backgrounds

without compare. She continues to do select freelance styling for the Meredith Corporation and Hearst Publications, as well as private design commissions.

Carla Scott is my pattern writer, technical editor, and general knitting wizard. Practically born into the business, she is without peer in her fabulous knowledge of knitting and garment structure, and for many years she has been able to translate my design concepts into written instructions and comprehensive charts. She lights up when presented with a new design challenge, figuring out details that practically make me faint. She is also a delight to work with, clear and calm amidst a mountain of math and engineering. Carla is senior editor at *Vogue Knitting* and, as always, has made working on this project a delight.

Judith Shangold is my pattern checker par excellence and has the enormous task of reviewing all the patterns and charts at many different stages for accuracy and consistency. A designer herself, Judith publishes under Designs by Judith and A Bear in Sheep's Clothing.

THE KNITTERS

Finding hand-knitters with an eye for perfection and professional craftsmanship is ever a challenge, but I always seem to do it! We often have knitting emergencies, last-minute changes, and reknits. Knitting under fire can be exacting at best, nerve-racking at worst. And in this book, for the first time I have adult garments as well as children's wear, and the resulting time warp was enormous. The time needed to

Carol Gillis, my studio assistant, is also a fabulous knitter, problem solver, and designer. **Starr Moore** knits nimbly and has also been known to figure out patterns. **Janice Bye, Connie Gemmer, Charlotte Parry, Veronica Manning, Ellen L'Esperance,** and **Leslie Scanlon** round out my band of intrepid and invaluable knitters. **Christina Astrachan** does the perfectly beautiful crocheted finishing.

knit or reknit an adult piece, rather than one for a 2 year old, is quite different to say the least!

Nita Young has fleet fingers, and she flies through even the most challenging pieces with ease. **Audrey Lewis** and **Lucinda Heller** are our Fair Isle masters, and their 2-color knitting is absolutely perfect. **Peggy Lewis** is our speed queen, knitting with more alacrity than I have ever seen, perfectly to boot. **Joan Cassidy** knits elegantly, with the most beautifully finished garments around.

MODELS

This book doubled the fun, literally, as we found *both* big and little fish to model this collection. I tried to find entire families or at least parent and child combos, although sometimes we substituted other combinations, with great success. This coterie of models was quite diverse, found everywhere from my friends and family to random meetings on the street! I am always on the lookout for new faces, and I look for spice and personality as well as beauty. After all the work to create this myriad collection, it is always a thrill to see the garments in real life on such charming models!

Cable Guy	Alexander Eaton and Luke Ford; Bionna Killian
Garter Cardi	Stephanie and Olivia Clifford
Striper	Stephanie and Meghan Clifford
Get Fleeced	Spencer Hoffman and Sam Kegan

Garter-T	Lily Hoffman and Montana Braxton
Furz	Petra Ledkovsky and Emma Dylan Henry-Tingle
Nordica	Steve McDavitt, Lucia Helder, and Carol Gillis
Chin Chin	Yueer and Jing Jing Ren, and Heidi Gerquest
Winter Argyle	Mark and Thomas Feenstra; Gail Henry
Festiva	Mabel Gerquest and Fiona Gerquest-Harbert
Ivy League	Peter and Meghan Clifford
Party Girl	Kirsten Scarcelli and Phoebe Min
Crew	Campbell and Thomas Badger
Bow Tie	Kirsten Scarcelli and Phoebe Min
Etc!	Carla and Patrice Scott; Connie and Fritz Gemmer; Judy, Alex, and Will Arbuckle; Isabel Smiles; and Gail Henry and Emma Dylan Henry-Tingle

Other enormous thanks go to my talented and ever-patient literary agent Sandy Taylor, to my extraordinary and esteemed editor Anne Knudsen, and to Lynda Litchfield, my graphic design mentor. Thanks also to my mother, Nancy Whipple Lord, for teaching me how to knit, and to my grandmother, Flora Whipple, for teaching *her* to knit.

And finally special thanks to Carol Gillis, my studio assistant. Working above and beyond, Carol not only keeps the studio organized and running smoothly, she also is a gifted knitter, saving the day one way or the other, sometimes even modeling, with enthusiasm and charm.

To everyone, bravo and merci!

Shopping Notes

All the beautiful yarns and products used in this book are available from the following distributors. You can contact them for shops in your area. These companies provide some of the most beautiful yarns on the market, and you can depend on them for the best. Always find the very best materials available, and you will love working on your projects.

YARNS

BERROCO
14 Elmdale Road
P.O. Box 367
Uxbridge, MA 01569-0367

BROWN SHEEP
100662 County Road 16
Mitchell, NE 69357
www.brownsheep.com

MANOS DEL URUGUAY
Design Source, U.S. Distributor
38 Montvale Avenue, Suite 145
Stoneham, MA 02180

ROWAN USA
5 Northern Boulevard
Amherst, NH 03031

CRYSTAL PALACE
3006 San Pablo Avenue
Berkeley, CA 94702

UNIQUE KOLOURS
1428 Oak Lane
Downington, PA 19335

REYNOLDS
c/o JCA
35 Scales Lane
Townsend, MA 01469-1094

NEEDLES

ADDI TURBOS
Skacel Collection, Inc.
224 S.W. 12th Street
Renton, WA 98055

SWALLOW CASEIN
Design Source
38 Montvale Avenue, Suite 145
Stoneham, MA 02180

CRYSTAL PALACE
3006 San Pablo Avenue
Berkeley, CA 94702

BUTTONS

ZECCA
P.O. Box 1664
Lakeville, CT 06039
(Hand-made polymer clay buttons)

CENTRAL YARN
53 Oak Street
Portland, ME 04101

MINNOWKNITS™ PATTERNS

Available at fine yarn shops and distributed by:
DESIGN SOURCE
P.O. Box 770
Medford, MA 02155
(781) 438-9631
shangold@usa.net
www.minnowknits.com

From My Bookshelf

Books on knitting abound, but I have found a few to be particularly wonderful, full of insight, technical information, and design inspiration.

Editors of *Vogue Knitting*. *Vogue Knitting*. New York: Pantheon Books, 1989.
> *One of my favorites, this book is rich in history and is great for technique, with clear illustrations for just about everything. It is required for my classes and has good basic design information and some traditional patterns. If you just buy one book, buy this.*

Hiatt, June Hemons. *The Principles of Knitting.* New York: Simon and Schuster, 1988.
> *This book is, unbelievably, out of print but is wonderful if you can find it!*

Goldberg, Rhoda Ochser. *The New Knitting Dictionary.* New York: Crown Publishers, 1984.

Newton, Deborah. *Designing Knitwear.* Newton, CT: Taunton Press, 1992.
> *This is a fabulous book on design, including history, technique, and new ways to see.*

Norbury, James, and Margaret Aguter. *Oldhams Encyclopedia of Knitting.* London: Oldhams Books, Ltd., 1957.

Standfield, Lesley. *The New Knitting Stitch Library.* Radnor, PA: Chilton Book Company, 1992.
> *This is comprehensive, with some new stitches for inspiration.*

Stanley, Montse. *The Handknitters Handbook.* London: David and Charles, 1986.
> *This book is a great source for various cast-on techniques.*

Square, Vicki. *The Knitter's Companion.* Loveland, CO: Interweave Press, 1996.
> *Tuck this into your knitting bag for a quick, convenient reference book.*

Zimmerman, Elizabeth. *Knitters Almanac.* New York: Dover Publications, 1981.

———. *Knitting Without Tears.* New York: Charles Scribner's Sons, 1971.

In Short

approx	approximately
beg	beginning
CC	contrasting color
cont	continue(s) or continuing
cn	cable needle
dec	decrease(s)
dpns	double pointed needles
est	established
foll	follows
inc(s)	increase(s)
k	knit
k2tog	knit 2 stitches together
MC	main color
p	purl
p2tog	purl 2 stitches together
pat(s)	pattern(s)
psso	pass slipped stitch over last stitch worked
rem	remaining
rep	repeat(s)
rev St st	reverse stockinette stitch, k all WS rows, p all RS rows

rib	rib(bing)
rnd(s)	round(s) in circular knitting
RS	right side
sl	slip, slipped, or slipping
st(s)	stitch(es)
St st	stockinette stitch, k all RS rows, p all WS rows
tog	together
WS	wrong side
yo	yarn over

Needle Conversions

Metric (mm)	US	Old UK
2	0	14
2.25	1	13
2.5		
2.75	2	12
3		
3.25	3	10
3.5	4	
3.75	5	
4	6	8
4.5	7	7
5	8	6
5.5	9	5
6	10	4
6.5	10.5	3
7		2
7.5		1
8	11	0
9	13	00
10	15	000